michel roux eggs

photography by Martin Brigdale

WILEY
John Wiley & Sons, Inc.

michel roux

eggs

All spoon measures are level unless otherwise stated: 1 tsp = 5ml spoon;1 tbsp = 15ml spoon.

Use fresh herbs, sea salt and freshly ground black pepper unless otherwise suggested.

Egg sizes are given where they are critical, otherwise use medium eggs, preferably organic or free-range. Anyone who is pregnant or in a vulnerable health group avoid recipes that use raw egg whites or lightly cooked eggs.

Timings are for fan-assisted ovens. If you are using a conventional oven, increase the temperature by 25°F (10°C). Use an oven thermometer to check the temperature.

Editorial director **Anne Furniss**
Creative director **Mary Evans**
Project editor **Janet Illsley**
Translator and editor **Kate Whiteman**
Photographer **Martin Brigdale**
Props stylist **Helen Trent**
Production **Rebecca Short**

First published in 2005 by Quadrille Publishing Limited, Alhambra House, 27-31 Charing Cross Road, London WC2H 0LS

Published by John Wiley & Sons, Inc., Hoboken, New Jersey
Published simultaneously in Canada

For general information about our other products and services, please contact our Customer Care Department within the United States at (800) 762-2974, outside the United States at (317) 572-3993 or fax (317) 572-4002.

Wiley also publishes its books in a variety of electronic formats. Some content that appears in print may not be available in electronic books. For more information about Wiley products, visit our web site at www.wiley.com.

Library of Congress Cataloging-in-Publication Data:
Roux, Michel, 1941-
Eggs / Michel Roux ; photography by Martin Brigdale.
p. cm.
Includes index.
ISBN 0-471-76913-4 (cloth)
1. Cookery (Eggs) 2. Eggs. I. Title.
TX745.R84 2005
641.6'75–dc22
2005018335

ISBN 0-471-76913-4

Printed in Singapore
10 9 8 7 6 5 4 3 2

introduction

I respect the egg for its genius in all forms of cooking. In my view, it is an undervalued food, invariably overshadowed by expensive, luxury ingredients. So, I have decided that it is time for me to write a book about this most fragile and defenseless of all foods, to bestow the egg with the honor it deserves.

Eggs have been much maligned over the past two decades, variously branded high in cholesterol, difficult to digest, carriers of salmonella, and the like. But, in reality, they are highly nutritious—and simple and quick to cook. An egg is a treasure chest of substances that are essential for a balanced diet—rich in proteins, lipids, vitamins and minerals, including iron and zinc. It provides first-class protein, is low in sodium, and a medium egg contains only 78 calories. Ideal for breakfast, lunch, tea, dinner, and supper, eggs are also great in sandwiches, an ideal picnic food, and they are essential in the preparation of so many different desserts, cakes, and sauces.

Eggs have always fascinated me. I love their oval, sometimes elongated shape, the purity of their lines, and the tint of their shells—ranging from natural white to pale nut-brown. When I hold an egg in my hand, I feel that it represents the image of the universe, and it awakens and increases my respect for life.

At the age of barely three, I would rush outside whenever I heard Julie, our family hen, cackling to announce that she was about to lay. I would gently collect the still warm new-laid egg and hurry to the kitchen with it. My mother collected the eggs in a large bowl, which would be kept full during the summer; in winter Julie laid only one or two eggs a week—but we loved her just the same.

Like bread, eggs are one of life's most basic and indispensable foods. I first started to discover their professional value when I began my pâtisserie apprenticeship at the age of fourteen. Since then, eggs have become my most faithful kitchen companions and they hold no secrets for me. In this book, I share their secrets with you, offering over 130 recipes and ideas for using eggs. Some are classic, others more modern and creative, but all reflect my personal style.

different kinds of eggs

Hen's eggs Throughout the world, these are by far the most common and widely eaten eggs. They are referred to simply as "eggs," whereas those laid by other birds are specifically named. Hen's eggs vary in weight from $2\frac{1}{4}$oz (53g) for a small egg to over $2\frac{3}{4}$oz (73g) for a very large one. You can buy lots of different types of hen's eggs; for more information, see page 12.

Bantam eggs Weighing 1–$1\frac{1}{2}$oz (30–40g), these are of equal quality to hen's eggs. Bantams hens are half the size of normal chickens, and their eggs are perfect for babies or dishes where eggs are best featured discreetly.

Duck eggs These weigh about $3\frac{1}{2}$oz (85–95g) and contain a little more fat than hen's eggs. I am very partial to their rich flavor, which is at its best in soft-cooked and scrambled eggs, omelets, and in desserts.

Goose eggs Weighing $6\frac{1}{2}$–7oz (180–200g), these have chalky-white, very hard shells, and a more pronounced flavor than hen's eggs. Usually I hard-cook and slice them into disks, cover them with a tomato or cheese sauce, and heat in the oven for a few minutes before serving. I use them for quiches or my leek flamiche (see page 201).

Pigeon eggs These only weigh about $\frac{1}{2}$oz (15g). They are perfectly pleasant, but nothing special. Indeed I think a pigeon tastes rather better than its egg...

Quail's eggs These attractive little speckled eggs weigh $\frac{1}{2}$–$\frac{3}{4}$oz (15–20g) and they can be cooked in the same way as hen's eggs, though for rather less time. The delicate, creamy texture and fine flavor of quail's eggs makes them very popular, but it is important to avoid overcooking them, even when hard-cooking. They are perfect for canapés and can be eaten in a single mouthful.

Ostrich eggs At the other end of the scale, these weigh 1lb 2oz–1lb 5oz (500–600g). At least the ostrich enabled me to take on the challenge of feeding six people with one egg, much to the amusement and astonishment of everyone! Ostrich eggs have a pronounced flavor, which needs to be tempered with flavorings like herbs or cheese. They can be used for omelets and in pâtisserie, but the shells are very hard and difficult to crack open.

Gull's eggs These are considered a delicacy in England, where it is only permitted to collect them from around the end of April to mid-May (the exact period varies, according to the weather). I love their flavor and prefer to semi hard-cook them very lightly, so that they remain soft in the middle. I serve them as an appetizer with celery salt or sweet paprika and buttered whole wheat bread. Gull's eggs are not cheap, but they justify their expense.

There are many other varieties of eggs that are less widely available but perfectly edible. Sometimes obtainable from farmers, poulterers, game dealers, and high-class grocery stores, they including the following:
Guinea fowl eggs Weighing 1oz (30g), these have a delicate flavor and are ideal as an appetizer or in a salad.
Pheasant eggs Weighing 1oz (30g), these have a strong flavor and are best served hard-cooked.
Emu eggs Weighing $\frac{3}{4}$–1lb (350–450g) and popular in Australia. Best scrambled, but can be used in pâtisserie.

Most wild bird's eggs are strictly protected by laws, which prohibit collecting or selling them commercially at any time, or only permit this at specified periods during the year. Contravention of these laws is severely penalized.

Eggshells are a natural barrier against germs and bacteria, which is ineffective if the shell is cracked or broken. I strongly advise you not to use eggs with damaged shells.

Never break eggs straight into a mixture or into the pan when cooking, but first crack them individually into a ramekin to check that they are fresh.

Eggs must be kept in a cool place, but should always be taken out of the refrigerator an hour or two before using. Store them in their cartons or in the egg compartment of the refrigerator with the pointed end downward to keep the yolk centered in the white.

Egg shells are porous, the yolks readily absorbing both good flavors and undesirable ones, so store eggs apart from any other foods unless you are imparting flavor.

To separate an egg, crack it open over a bowl and pass the yolk between the two half shells, allowing the egg white to fall into the bowl. Separated egg whites can be kept for several days in an airtight container in the refrigerator, or frozen for a few weeks.

facts about eggs

Labeling of eggs This varies from country to country. In the US, most hen's eggs are classified according to their quality and size under specific US Department of Agriculture (USDA) standards. The USDA shield on the packaging shows that the eggs have been federally inspected. Eggs are graded from AA, A, and B according to both exterior and interior quality and all eggs sold must meet grade B or higher. Special breed hen's eggs are available from supermarkets, farmer's markets, and other specialist suppliers. These often have a denser texture, superior flavor, and larger, deeper colored yolks.

Organic eggs These are increasingly available. They are produced by hens fed on natural feed (free from additives), which have freedom to roam outdoors and are kept in relatively small flocks. Free-range eggs are produced by hens that also have continuous access to outdoor runs, and a varied diet, though they are usually kept in larger flocks. I advocate the use of these eggs, whenever possible.

Eggshell color This varies according to the breed of chicken. American consumers favor eggs with a white shell, whereas the French and British are more inclined to prefer brown eggs. Some special breed hens produce eggs with pretty colored shells in a range of pastel shades.

The flavor of an egg This is concentrated in the yolk and is determined by what the chicken eats—corn, wheat, etc. Its rich taste is composed of many different elements. Needless to say, you cannot identify these individually when you taste an egg.

Egg sizes Hen's eggs vary in weight and range from ½oz (15g) per dozen for peewee eggs, 18oz (510g) per dozen for small, 21oz (600g) per dozen for medium, 24oz (680g) per dozen for large, 27oz (765g) per dozen for extra large, and 30oz (850g) per dozen for jumbo. The only inedible part of an egg is the shell, which weighs about ⅓oz (9g). Of the edible parts of a medium egg, the white weighs about 1oz (33g) and the yolk approximately ¾oz (20g).

Egg whites These are a vital ingredient in soufflés, mousses, and meringues, their whisked texture lending extraordinary volume and lightness. Unlike the yolks, egg whites vary significantly according to the size of the egg. I almost always use the whites of medium eggs. If you are unsure, it is best to measure the volume of egg whites: A generous 1 cup (250ml)= 8 medium egg whites; 2 cups (500ml)= 16 whites.
In many sauces, pastries, and other recipes, only the egg yolks are used, and the whites are simply thrown away. This is completely unnecessary, particularly as egg whites freeze extremely well. In fact, they become more glutinous on freezing, which makes them even better for preparing meringues and soufflés.

Freshness If you are in any doubt about the freshness of an egg, do the following simple test: Drop the egg into cold water salted (⅜ cup (100g) salt to 4 cups (1 liter) water). If the egg sinks, it is "extra fresh;" if it remains suspended in the water, it is about 2 weeks old; if it floats, the egg is not fresh enough to be eaten and should be thrown away.

Did you know? A single hen lays around 280 eggs each year. Light, temperature, and feed all affect her laying capacity. She needs at least 12 hours of light to conceive an egg and the time between conception and laying is a mere 24–26 hours. And finally, I should mention that a hen has no need of a male mate to conceive an egg, which can be produced from a fertilized or unfertilized ovum.

At The Waterside Inn, I use free-range eggs from a local farm. They are supremely fresh, with beautiful deep yellow yolks. I recommend that you buy organic or free-range eggs whenever possible. Those labeled "extra fresh" guarantee that the eggs have been laid within the past 9 days. "Fresh" eggs have been laid within 28 days.

A good-quality nonstick skillet will make all the difference when you are cooking omelets, fried eggs, crêpes, etc. I use Tefal pans, which give excellent results at both low and high temperatures.

Use a large balloon whisk or a hand-held electric beater to whisk egg whites and make sure the bowl and whisk are clean and dry. Even a trace of grease, water, or egg yolk will prevent the egg whites from reaching their maximum volume. Whisked egg whites should stand in soft peaks—avoid overwhisking.

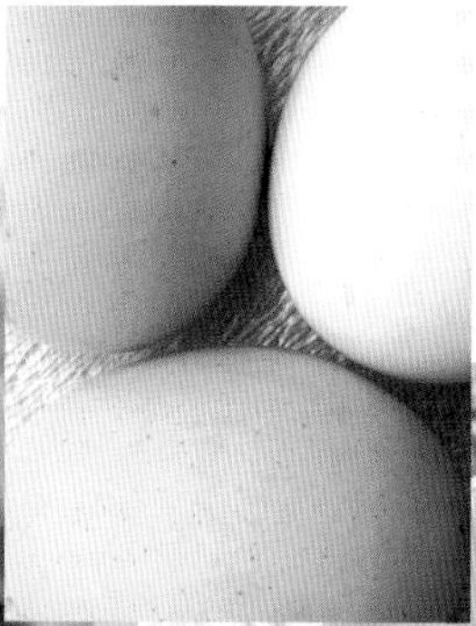

Very carefully fold whisked egg whites into a mixture, to avoid losing volume.

The first six chapters of this book showcase eggs as a dish in their own right, covering all the different ways of cooking an egg—boiling, poaching, frying, scrambling, baking, and omelets. The recipes in the subsequent chapters use the amazing culinary properties of eggs to create a variety of dishes, including appetizers, snacks, main courses, desserts, and sauces. Eggs are not necessarily the main ingredient here, but their unique properties are essential to the dish: soufflés, custards, ice creams, meringues, sponges, and much more...

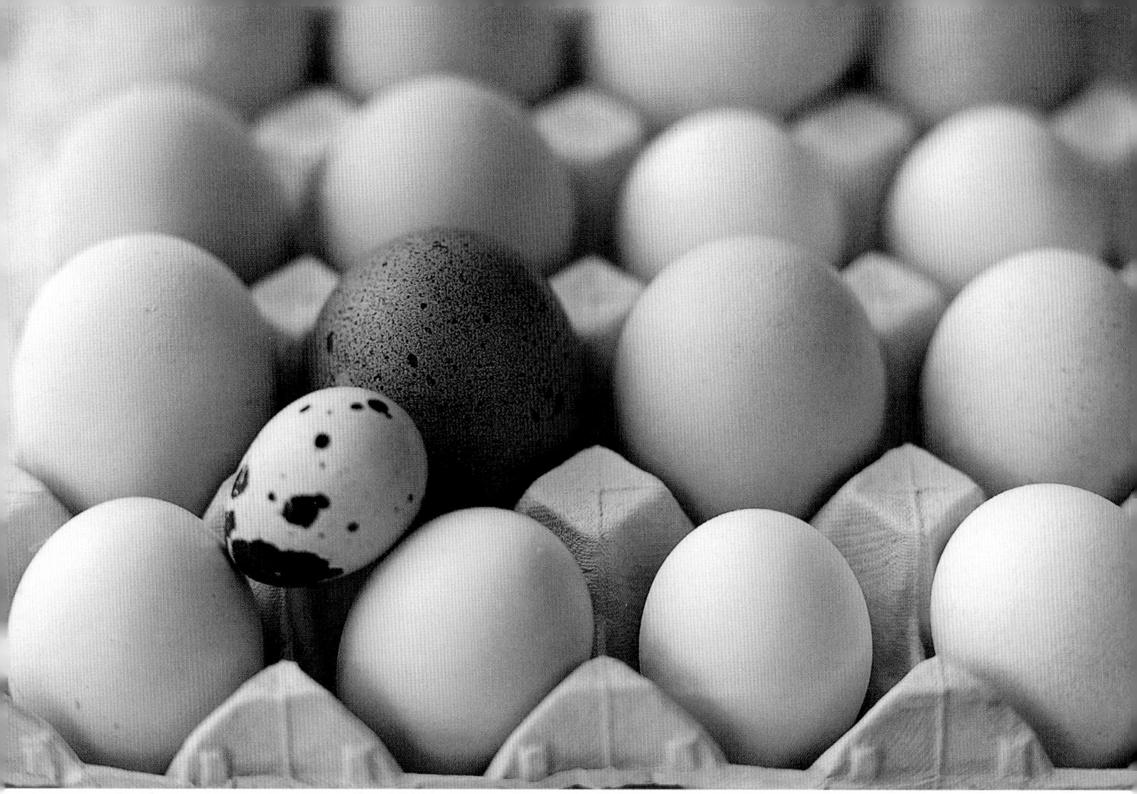

boiled eggs

Simplicity is the essence of this chapter, for the egg is not only cooked in its shell, but often served in it too. It is essential to use very fresh eggs, especially if they are to be soft-cooked. I have used the same technique for boiling eggs (see page 18) since I was eighteen. It requires neither a watch nor an egg timer and it is infallible—once you've tried it, I am sure you will adopt it forever. Mollet eggs make delectable appetizers. I love to add them to an arugula or dandelion salad, and when I'm in the South of France, I enjoy them in tomato nests with crunchy cucumber (see page 31). Hard-cooked eggs have many uses, but they must be boiled carefully, to ensure that they don't become rubbery. I always cook them in barely simmering water at 158°F (70°C) to keep the texture supple. They are perfect for a quick snack or a picnic.

boiled eggs

Take the eggs out of the refrigerator about 2 hours in advance to prevent them from cracking when the water boils. Or pierce the rounded end of the shell with a pin, to allow air to escape during cooking. Use a pan large enough for all the eggs to lie comfortably. If they knock each other during cooking, the shells may crack and some white will escape.

soft-cooked eggs

Put the eggs in a pan, cover generously with cold water, and set over medium heat. As soon as the water comes to a boil, count up to 60 seconds for a medium egg; the egg white will be lightly set. If you prefer the white slightly firmer but the yolk still runny, cook the egg for another 30 seconds. For an even firmer white with the yolk just beginning to set, allow 30 seconds more ($1\frac{1}{2}$ minutes in total). As soon as the eggs are cooked to your liking, lift them out of the water or they will continue to cook. Serve in egg cups as soon as possible. Take off the tops by tapping the pointed end with a sharp knife.

mollet eggs
Boil as for soft-cooked eggs, but allow only 3 minutes once the water starts simmering. As soon as the water boils, lower the heat, otherwise if the eggs cook in fast-boiling water the whites will become rubbery. As soon as the eggs are cooked, use a slotted spoon to transfer them to a bowl of very cold water with some ice cubes. Let cool for about 10 minutes, then tap the shells with the back of a spoon to crack them. To shell the eggs, start at the rounded end where the little air sac is, and peel off the shells under a trickle of cold running water. The water will infiltrate between the solid egg white and the membrane that lines the shell, making it easier to peel the egg without damaging it.

hard-cooked eggs
Boil exactly as for mollet eggs, but cook for 6 minutes after the water starts simmering.

Serve soft-cooked eggs with a selection of delicate flavorings, leaving everyone to mix their preferred ingredients into their egg. Allow 2 eggs per person—they are bound to be popular, especially if you serve them on a large platter for brunch. Or why not push the boat out and serve them for breakfast in bed with a ramekin of caviar....

Mini-ratatouille Cut a medium onion, a small chunk of red, yellow, or green bell pepper, a small zucchini, a dwarf eggplant, and a very ripe, skinned tomato into $^{1}/_{8}$-inch (3–4-mm) dice. Gently heat 3 tbsp olive oil in a small pan, sweat the onion for 2 minutes, then add the bell pepper and cook for 5 minutes. Add the zucchini, then at 2-minute intervals, add the eggplant and tomato. Season with salt and pepper, add a few thyme leaves, and serve just warm.

Olives Choose a few different green and black olives. Pit them, chop larger olives, and mix together.

Mini-croutons Cut the crusts off a slice of white bread and cut the bread into tiny cubes. Heat a little oil or unsalted butter in a skillet and fry the croutons over medium heat until golden. Drain well on paper towels and serve warm.

Capers The small ones are best. Rinse off the vinegar under cold running water and drain well.

Soft fresh herbs Choose whichever soft herbs you like and snip them finely. My favorites are chervil, Italian parsley, and chives.

Grated cheese There is nothing better than freshly grated Comté or Parmesan.

Salt and pepper Freshly milled sea salt and cracked pepper are essential.

Here is an army of little soldiers to delight the eye and palate. They are all delicious dipped into soft-cooked eggs. Allow 1 or 2 soft-cooked eggs per person.

Asparagus tips Peel the stalks with a vegetable peeler, and cook the asparagus for a few minutes in boiling salted water until done to your liking (they are best cooked until firm but not crunchy).

Grissini Wrap them in thin slices of prosciutto or Bayonne ham just before serving.

French fries Cut the potatoes into thin fries and deep-fry until very crisp on the outside but still soft in the middle. Drain on paper towels and serve piping hot.

Cheese straws Use ready-made cheese straws, or buy some puff pastry and make your own. Serve warm.

Carrot sticks Peel a few carrots and cut them into very thick, long sticks. Blanch in boiling salted water with a pinch of curry powder and a little bit of butter added for 30 seconds. Drain well and serve just warm or cold.

Brochettes of Comté or Gruyère cheese To make rosemary skewers, strip the leaves from some fairly woody rosemary stems, leaving a sprig of leaves at the top of each one. Cut the cheese into small cubes and thread 5 or 6 cubes onto each rosemary skewer (from the bare end). If necessary, first make a hole through the cheese cubes with a toothpick.

soft-cooked eggs with vanilla caramel & brioche

serves 4

4 medium eggs
1 vanilla bean, split lengthwise
4 slices of brioche loaf
for the caramel sauce
$^{1}/_{2}$ cup (100g) superfine sugar
1 tsp lemon juice

A day in advance, put the raw eggs in an airtight container with the split vanilla bean, and refrigerate for 24 hours. The flavor of the vanilla will permeate the egg shells.

To make the caramel, put the sugar in a heavy, deep pan and dissolve over gentle heat, stirring constantly. As soon as it turns to a light caramel color, turn off the heat and pour in about $^{1}/_{3}$ cup (100 ml) boiling water and the lemon juice. Take care as the caramel is liable to splutter and spit. Stir the caramel with a small whisk and cook over medium heat for 2 to 3 minutes, until it has a syrupy consistency. With the tip of a knife, scrape in a few seeds from the vanilla bean. Pour into a small pitcher and keep at room temperature.

Toast the brioche slices, remove the crusts, and cut into soldiers; keep warm.

Soft-cook the eggs (see page 18) the way you like them, and put them into egg cups. Eat with a teaspoon, letting everyone drizzle some caramel over their egg and dip their brioche soldiers into the soft yolks.

"For anyone with a sweet tooth, this is breakfast heaven. Be prepared to cook extra eggs as they are addictive! Add a pinch of salt to the caramel for an interesting salty-sweet flavor."

mollet eggs with arugula & parmesan shavings

serves 4

"If you are using wild arugula, which has a more peppery flavor than the cultivated variety, you may prefer to add a little oak leaf lettuce to soften the flavor."

14oz (400g) arugula leaves
6 tbsp Swiss vinaigrette (see page 296)
4 medium eggs
4oz (100g) Parmesan, shaved into curls

Wash the arugula in cold water, drain, and keep cool. Dress the arugula with the vinaigrette and divide between 4 plates.

Cook the mollet eggs (see page 19) and shell them. Cut the eggs in half lengthwise and arrange on the arugula salad. Scatter on the Parmesan shavings and serve.

illustrated on previous page

mollet egg & zucchini tarts with spinach sabayon

serves 4

7oz (200g) tart pie dough (see page 194), or use ready-made basic pie dough
flour, to dust
5oz (150g) zucchini, cut into thick sticks
1/4 cup (50ml) olive oil
1 garlic clove, unpeeled and halved
1 thyme sprig
4 medium eggs
1 tsp snipped basil leaves
salt and freshly ground pepper
1 quantity spinach & watercress sabayon (see page 293)

To make the pastry shells, roll out the dough on a lightly floured surface to an 1/8 inch (3mm) thickness and cut out four 4-inch (10-cm) circles, with a pastry cutter. Use these to line 4 tartlet pans, about 2 3/4 inches (7cm) diameter (see page 196). Refrigerate for 30 minutes. Meanwhile, preheat the oven to 400°F (200°C).

Prick the bottom of each pastry shell several times with a fork, line with a disk of waxed paper and fill with baking beans or dried beans. Bake blind for 10 minutes, then remove the beans and paper, lower the oven setting to 350°F (180°C), and bake for another 5 minutes. Unmold and keep at room temperature.

Put the zucchini in a small pan with the olive oil, garlic, and thyme, and cook very gently for 4 to 5 minutes. Remove the garlic and thyme, and leave the zucchini in the oil at room temperature.

Cook the mollet eggs (see page 19) but don't shell them.

Drain the zucchini thoroughly, then mix with the basil and seasoning to taste. Divide between the pastry shells. Put the mollet eggs in a bowl, cover with boiling water for 30 seconds, then drain and shell. Place a mollet egg in each pastry shell. Arrange on warm plates, coat with the sabayon, and serve, as an appetizer.

illustrated on page 292

mollet eggs in tomato nests with crunchy cucumber

serves 4

"All the ingredients for this easy appetizer can be prepared in advance and assembled at the last moment. The refreshing crunchy cucumber contrasts well with the tomato."

4 beefsteak tomatoes, about 7oz (200g) each
salt
1 cucumber, about 14oz (400g)
4 medium eggs
1¾ cups (400ml) bagnarotte sauce (see page 285)
4 chervil sprigs

for the marinade
⅔ cup (150ml) white wine vinegar
⅓ cup (75g) superfine sugar
few rosemary needles
pinch of salt and freshly ground pepper

First make the marinade. Put all the ingredients in a pan with about 3 tbsp (40ml) water, bring to a boil, then strain through a chinois or fine strainer into a bowl. Keep at room temperature.

To skin the tomatoes, make a slit in the top and cut out the cores. Plunge the tomatoes into boiling water for 10 to 15 seconds, until the skins starts to split, refresh in ice water, then peel off the skins. Cut a sliver off the bottom of each tomato so that they stand upright. Slice off the tops and scoop out the flesh and seeds with a spoon. Season the insides with salt, invert onto paper towels, and let drain.

Using a vegetable peeler, peel the cucumber along its length on one side only. Cut a bit off both ends. Using a mandolin, shave the skin side of the cucumber into 1/16-inch (2-mm) thick ribbons and place in the marinade. Seed the other half of the cucumber and finely dice the flesh. Add to the marinade with the ribbons, leave for 3 minutes, then drain.

Cook the mollet eggs (see page 19) and shell them. Mix a little bagnarotte sauce into the diced cucumber and divide between the tomatoes. Put a cucumber ribbon into each tomato, leaving the border overhanging the top. Put a mollet egg into each nest, coat lavishly with bagnarotte sauce, top with a sprig of chervil, and serve.

mollet eggs on crabmeat & celeriac julienne

serves 4

1 celeriac, about 1lb (450g)
1 quantity Swiss vinaigrette (see page 296)
9oz (250g) fresh white crabmeat
juice of ½ lemon
salt and freshly ground pepper
4 medium eggs
1 tender lettuce heart, about 8 leaves
½ lemon, cut into 4 wedges
2 tbsp Italian parsley leaves

Peel the celeriac with a sharp knife, discarding all the hard bits, and cut into julienne on a mandolin. Toss with 4 tbsp Swiss vinaigrette and keep at room temperature.

Check the crabmeat carefully, removing any cartilage and fragments of shell. Mix the crabmeat with the lemon juice and season with salt and pepper to taste.

Cook the mollet eggs (see page 19) and shell them.

Divide the celeriac between 4 plates. Pile the crabmeat in a dome in the center and top with the eggs. Arrange a couple of lettuce leaves, a lemon wedge, and some parsley on one side. Drizzle a little vinaigrette over the eggs and serve the rest separately. Serve chilled.

"You can use frozen or canned crabmeat for this appetizer, but fresh crab has a superior flavor."

"I truly adore this regal and scrumptious sandwich with its medley of hot and cold filling ingredients. My wife, Robyn, makes it as a surprise treat on my days off, or on vacation. You can vary the ingredients—substitute raw or cooked ham or hot bacon for the eel, for example."

hard-cooked egg & smoked eel ciabatta sandwich

serves 4

1 ciabatta loaf, about 11 x 4 inches (28 x 10cm)
$^2/_3$ cup (150g) mayonnaise (see page 282), or use ready-made
scant $^1/_4$ cup (50g) pesto (see page 211), or use ready-made
8 tbsp (100g) butter, softened
salt and freshly ground pepper

for the filling
2 oz (50g) baby spinach, shredded
4 oz (100g) smoked eel, thinly sliced
4 oz (100g) tomatoes, thinly sliced
1 avocado, pitted, peeled, and thinly sliced
4 hard-cooked eggs (see page 19)
$^3/_4$ cup (50g) snipped chives
4 oz (100g) cucumber, peeled and sliced
1 tbsp basil leaves
5 oz (150g) mozzarella, thinly sliced
2 oz (50g) Cheddar or Gruyère, grated

Put the ciabatta on a board and slice it lengthwise, with a serrated knife, two-thirds above the base to make a sort of long lid. Using the knife and scraping with a fork, remove a little of the soft crumb from the lid and two-thirds from the base. Mix the mayonnaise with the pesto and set aside.

Preheat the broiler. Spread the softened butter all over the inside of the ciabatta and season lightly with salt and pepper. Broil the base and lid until almost golden. Layer all the filling ingredients into the base, in the order listed above, placing the eggs lengthwise and pressing each layer lightly with your fingertips. Spread half the mayonnaise/pesto mixture over the spinach layer, and the rest over the basil leaves. Finish with a layer of mozzarella slices, topped with the grated cheese.

Place the filled ciabatta base under the broiler for 5 to 6 minutes. Reheat the cut side of the lid for 2 minutes. Replace the lid on the ciabatta base, pressing down lightly with your fingertips. Use a palette knife to slide the ciabatta onto a board and present it whole at the table before cutting it into slices with a knife to serve.

mini scotch eggs

serves 4

8 quail's eggs
10oz (300g) pork tenderloin or picnic shoulder, trimmed and finely ground
1 egg white
2 tsp snipped parsley and chives
salt and freshly ground pepper
small pinch of cayenne
flour, to dust
2 medium eggs
2 tbsp milk
$^1/_2$ cup (100g) fine white bread crumbs, to coat
$1^1/_4$ cups (300ml) peanut oil, to deep-fry

Hard-cook the quail's eggs (see page 19), allowing $2^1/_2$ to 3 minutes after the water starts simmering. Shell and pat dry with paper towels.

In a bowl, mix the pork with the egg white, parsley, chives, salt, pepper, and cayenne. Take about an eighth of this mixture and lightly flatten it in the palm of your hand. Place a boiled quail's egg in the middle and gently mold the forcemeat around the egg; it should not more than $^1/_8$ inch (4mm) thick. Repeat with the other quail's eggs.

Season the flour with salt and pepper and scatter on a board. Beat the eggs with the milk and season with salt and pepper. Roll the Scotch eggs in the seasoned flour, taking care not to spoil the shape, and dust off any excess. Dip each one into the egg mixture, then roll in bread crumbs to coat evenly.

Heat the oil for deep-frying in a deep pan to 350°F (180°C). Fry the eggs, a few at a time, for $1^1/_2$ to 2 minutes. Lift out with a slotted spoon and drain on paper towels.

"These are best eaten slightly warm as an appetizer, or serve them cold for a picnic or as canapés. A garnish of raw or deep-fried celery leaves is perfect. Serve mayonnaise or a spicy relish on the side."

hard-cooked eggs stuffed with mussels

serves 4

32 mussels, scrubbed
$^1/_4$ cup (50ml) dry white wine
4 hard-cooked eggs (see page 19)
$^2/_3$ cup (150g) mayonnaise (see page 282)
2 tbsp lemon juice
salt and freshly ground pepper
3 tbsp peanut oil
7 oz (200g) carrots, peeled and cut into julienne
$^1/_2$ red onion, finely chopped

Put the mussels and wine in a pan, cover with a tight-fitting lid, and cook for a few minutes until the shells have steamed opened. Lift out the mussels, shell them, and place in a bowl, discarding any that have not opened. Strain the cooking juices through a cheesecloth-lined strainer into the bowl. Keep at room temperature.

Cut the hard-cooked eggs in half lengthwise and carefully remove the yolks. Press the yolks through a coarse strainer to make egg mimosa.

Drain the mussels thoroughly, straining the juices into a pan. Reduce over low heat to a syrupy consistency. Cool, then stir into the mayonnaise. Mix in the mussels and arrange 3 or 4 mussels in each egg white cavity.

Put the lemon juice in a bowl with some salt and pepper, then whisk in the oil. Mix in the carrot julienne and chopped onion. Spoon onto a platter, arrange the stuffed eggs on top, and sprinkle with egg mimosa. Serve cold, but not chilled.

Alternative fillings
Broiled squid finely diced and mixed with my bagnarotte sauce (see page 285), served with a garnish of salmon eggs.
Brown shrimp mixed with finely diced boiled potatoes, flavored with Caesar dressing (see page 294), and generously sprinkled with snipped chives.

herb salad with hard-cooked eggs & tuna brochettes

serves 4

"I've used goose eggs for his modern version of a salade niçoise, but duck eggs or ordinary hen's eggs work equally well"

2 goose eggs (or 4 duck or hen's eggs)
1 tsp yellow mustard seeds

for the tuna brochettes

2 green bell peppers
about 1¼lb (560g) fresh tuna fillet
3 tbsp olive oil

for the herb salad

2 tbsp white wine vinegar
salt and freshly ground pepper
6 tbsp peanut oil
1½oz (40g) Italian parsley leaves
¾oz (20g) chervil sprigs
20 chives, cut into short lengths
1 shallot, finely chopped

Hard-cook the eggs (see page 19), allowing 12 minutes for goose eggs after the water starts simmering. Shell and cut into quarters.

For the brochettes, skin the green bell peppers with a potato peeler, cut into quarters, and remove the white membrane and seeds. Cut the flesh into 1¼-inch (3-cm) squares, blanch in boiling water for 1 minute, then drain. Cut the tuna into 12 cubes and brush lightly with olive oil. Thread the peppers and tuna alternately onto 4 skewers, starting and finishing with a bell pepper square.

For the herb salad, mix the wine vinegar, a little salt and pepper, and the oil in a bowl, then delicately mix in the herbs and shallot.

Heat a stovetop grill pan or griddle until very hot. Add the brochettes and sear on one side for 45 seconds or so, to mark a lattice marking. Repeat on every side, cooking for a total of 3 to 4 minutes for tuna that is still pink in the middle.

Divide the salad between 4 plates and arrange a tuna brochette on top. Place the hard-cooked egg quarters alongside and sprinkle with mustard seeds to serve.

poached eggs

From breakfast to lunch and through to supper, poached eggs are a real treat. Serve them plain or with a sauce, on toast, floating in a soup, or sitting atop my onion tartlets (see page 58). It is easy to poach eggs neatly draped in their whites, and it takes only 5 minutes of your time. A word of advice—don't add salt to the water as it hinders the white compacting and studs it with tiny holes. In 1982, my brother Albert and I accepted the challenge to cook a dinner for 3,500 people at the Royal Albert Hall. The first course was a classic Roux Brothers' dish *oeuf poché Albert*, comprising artichoke bases, smoked salmon mousse, and poached eggs, topped with a slice of smoked salmon. It took a brigade of four chefs led by my nephew, Michel Roux Junior, a day and a half to poach 3,500 eggs to perfection—truly the stuff of nightmares!

poached eggs

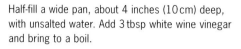

Half-fill a wide pan, about 4 inches (10 cm) deep, with unsalted water. Add 3 tbsp white wine vinegar and bring to a boil.

Break an egg into a ramekin or small bowl and tip it gently into the pan, at the point where the water is bubbling.

Repeat with the other eggs, but do not poach more than 4 eggs at a time. Poach for about $1\frac{1}{2}$ minutes.

Poached eggs are usually eaten as soon as they are ready, but they can be cooked ahead and kept in cold water in the refrigerator for up to 2 days. To reheat, immerse the poached eggs in a bowl of boiling water for 30 seconds only.

Using a slotted spoon or small skimmer, lift out the first egg and press the outside edge lightly to check if it is properly cooked.

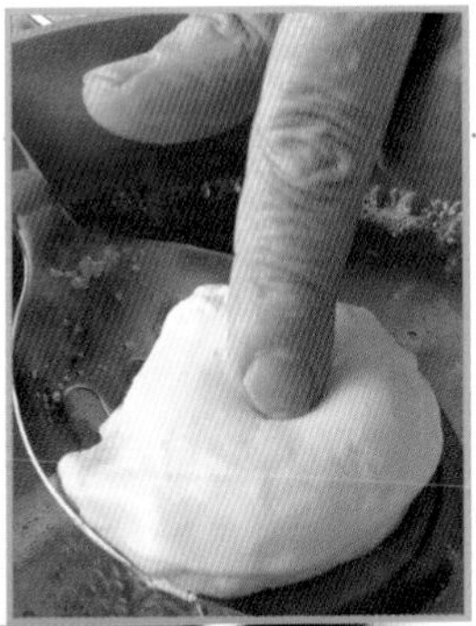

As soon as the egg is cooked to your liking, remove it with the skimmer or slotted spoon. Either serve immediately, or transfer to a bowl of ice water and leave for about 10 minutes.

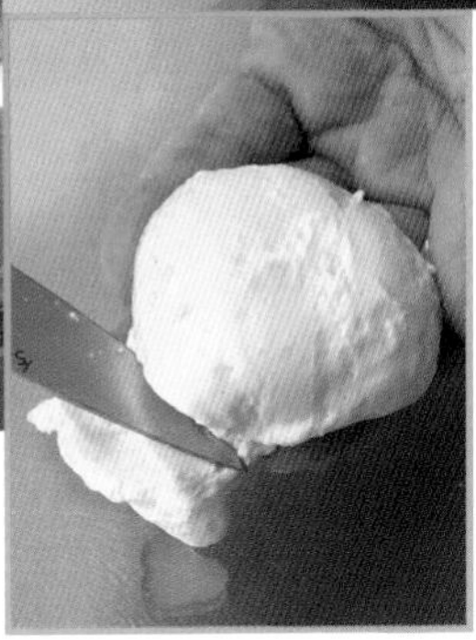

Trim the edges with a small knife to make a neat shape. This will also cut off the excess white that inevitably spreads during cooking. The poached egg is now ready.

eggs benedict

serves 4

2 English muffins
8 tbsp (100g) butter
4oz (100g) spinach, washed and stalks removed
salt and freshly ground pepper
4 small slices of cured tongue or ham
4 poached eggs (see page 44)
1 cup (200ml) hollandaise sauce (see page 278)
few chives, snipped into short lengths

Split the muffins and toast them lightly for a minute or two. Keep warm.

Heat 4 tbsp (50 g) butter in a skillet and cook the spinach for 1 to 2 minutes, until just wilted. Season with salt and pepper and keep warm. Heat the rest of the butter in the same pan and warm the tongue or ham slices for 1 to 2 minutes.

Immerse the poached eggs in boiling water for no more than 30 seconds to warm through, then drain thoroughly.

Put half a muffin on each plate and top with a slice of tongue or ham, some spinach, and a hot poached egg. Coat generously with hollandaise sauce, sprinkle with chives, and serve immediately, with the rest of the hollandaise sauce served separately.

"Ham is often substituted for tongue in this classic recipe, which is best eaten for brunch or as an appetizer."

eggs florentine

serves 4

$4\frac{1}{2}$tbsp (60g) butter
1lb 5oz (600g) spinach, washed and stalks removed
2 pinches of sugar
salt and freshly ground pepper
$\frac{1}{4}$ cup (50ml) heavy cream
freshly grated nutmeg
2oz (50g) Comté or Parmesan, freshly grated
1 cup (250g) hot Mornay sauce (see page 299)
4 poached eggs (see page 44)

In a skillet over high heat, melt half the butter. As soon as it has melted, add half the spinach and sprinkle with a pinch each of sugar and salt. Give the spinach a stir and cook for 1 minute, until just wilted, then tip into a colander and drain well. Repeat with the rest of the butter and spinach. Put the drained spinach in a pan, add the cream, season with a pinch of nutmeg, salt, and pepper, and keep warm.

When ready to serve, divide the spinach between 4 egg dishes or crème brûlée dishes and place in a low oven to keep warm. Preheat the broiler. Mix half of the grated cheese into the Mornay sauce. Put the poached eggs in a bowl and cover them with boiling water for 30 seconds. Drain well and place on top of the spinach in the dishes.

Coat the hot poached eggs generously with the sauce, then scatter over the rest of the cheese and pop under the hot broiler until it turns light nut-brown. Serve piping hot.

"There are three elements to success here—the quality of the spinach, a good Mornay sauce preferably with Comté cheese, and perfectly poached eggs. For a tempting variation, replace the cheese with mushrooms."

poached eggs with shrimp & confit tomatoes

serves 4

10oz (300g) cooked shrimp in the shell
½tsp curry powder
scant 1 cup (200g) mayonnaise (see page 282)
salt and freshly ground pepper
1 quantity confit tomatoes (see page 144)
1 avocado
juice of 1 lemon
4 poached eggs (see page 44)

Shell all the shrimp, leaving eight with their heads still attached for the garnish; set these aside. Dissolve the curry powder in 1 tbsp warm water, then add to the mayonnaise, mixing thoroughly with a whisk. Delicately mix in the shrimp and season with salt and pepper to taste.

Cut the confit tomatoes into ½-inch (1-cm) wide strips. Peel the avocado with a knife and cut into quarters, discarding the pit. Thinly slice each quarter, keeping it intact at one end, then fan out and sprinkle with a few drops of lemon juice.

To serve, divide the shrimp in mayonnaise between 4 plates, top each serving with a poached egg, and arrange an avocado fan on top. Scatter the confit tomato strips around the shrimp and garnish the edge of the plates with the whole shrimp.

"All the elements of this appetizer can be prepared a day ahead and simply arranged on the plates at the last moment."

poached eggs on potatoes with smoked haddock

serves 4

10oz (300g) piece smoked haddock fillet
$^3/_4$lb (350g) small new potatoes, preferably purple, washed
salt and freshly ground pepper
$2^1/_2$ cups (600ml) milk
1 small bouquet garni
3 tbsp (40g) butter, plus extra to grease
about $3^1/_4$oz (80g) shallots, finely chopped
4 poached eggs (see page 44)
$1^1/_4$ cups (300ml) sauce écossaise (page 297)

Soak the smoked haddock in cold water for 30 minutes. Put the potatoes in a pan, cover with cold water, and add salt. Boil gently for 20 minutes or until tender when pierced with a knife tip. Pour a little cold water into the pan to stop the cooking process and let cool. When cold, peel and slice the potatoes.

Drain the fish, place in a pan, and pour on the milk to cover, adding a little cold water if needed. Add the bouquet garni. Slowly bring to a simmer and poach gently for 5 minutes. Let the haddock cool in the milk until almost cold.

Heat the oven to 315°F (160°C). Melt the butter in a small pan, add the shallots, and sweat gently for 2 minutes. Grease 4 individual gratin or egg dishes generously with butter. Mix the shallots with the sliced potatoes and divide between the dishes, then flake the haddock over the top. Cover with foil and heat in the oven for 5 minutes.

Meanwhile, reheat the poached eggs in boiling water for no more than 30 seconds. Drain thoroughly and put a poached egg on top of the potatoes in each dish. Coat with piping hot sauce écossaise and serve. Accompany with a watercress or arugula salad for a light lunch.

herby poached eggs in mousseline potato nests

serves 4

10oz (300g) potatoes, preferably Russet Burbank or round white
salt
about $^2/_3$ cup (150ml) milk
3 tbsp (40g) butter
4 poached eggs (see page 44)
2 tbsp snipped soft herbs (parsley, chervil, chives)
roast chicken or pork pan juices, skimmed

Peel the potatoes, cut into pieces, and place in a pan. Cover with cold water, add a pinch of salt, and cook at a gentle boil for about 20 minutes until tender when pierced with a knife tip. Drain the potatoes and rub through a mouli or strainer into a pan.

Bring the milk to a boil. Place the potatoes over low heat and, with a wooden spoon, mix in the butter, then the boiling milk. Season to taste with salt.

Warm the poached eggs in boiling water for 30 seconds, drain well, and roll them in the snipped herbs.

Divide the potato between 4 deep plates and make a well in the center with the back of a spoon. Put a poached egg in each well and pour the warm chicken or pork juices round the eggs and all round the potatoes. Serve immediately.

illustrated on previous page

caesar salad with poached eggs

serves 4

"This delicious salad, with the addition of a poached egg, makes the perfect light lunch, dinner, or snack. To enjoy it at its best, serve the salad very cold, but not chilled."

12 canned white anchovy fillets
a little milk, to soak (optional)
2 romaine lettuces, trimmed
2 slices of white bread
4½tbsp (60g) peanut oil
½ quantity Caesar dressing (see page 294)
4oz (100g) Parmesan, in one piece
4 poached eggs (see page 44)
2tbsp chopped curly parsley

If necessary, soak the anchovy fillets in cold milk for 30 minutes to remove excess salt. Discard the greenest outer leaves from the lettuces. Cut the rest into 1½-inch (4-cm) chunks, wash in cold water, and drain thoroughly. Keep in the refrigerator.

To make the croutons, remove the crusts from the bread, then cut into ½-inch (1-cm) cubes. Heat the oil in a skillet and fry the bread cubes, turning, until golden all over. Drain in a colander, then on paper towels.

Put the lettuce into a large bowl, pour the dressing over, and mix delicately but thoroughly. Pile the lettuce into 4 deep plates. Scatter on the croutons and arrange 3 anchovy fillets on each salad. Finely shave the Parmesan over the salad, using a vegetable peeler.

Roll the poached eggs in the chopped parsley and place one in the middle of each salad. Serve immediately.

illustrated on page 295

poached egg in a light vegetable soup

serves 6–8

"This healthy, nourishing soup is quick to make and always popular with guests. Make sure you use ripe, flavorful tomatoes."

$2\frac{1}{4}$lb (1kg) very ripe tomatoes
1 lettuce, about 14oz (400g)
$4\frac{1}{2}$tbsp (60g) butter
$6\frac{1}{3}$ cups (1.25 liters) water or chicken stock
5oz (150g) potatoes, peeled and diced
salt and freshly ground pepper
6–8 poached eggs (see page 44)

Skin, quarter, and seed the tomatoes. Dice some of the tomato flesh or cut into diamonds; you need a spoonful for each serving; set aside. Trim the lettuce and wash it in cold water. Finely shred 2 or 3 leaves and keep with the reserved tomato. Shred the rest of the lettuce.

To make the soup, melt the butter in a pan, add the shredded lettuce, and sweat over medium heat for 3 or 4 minutes. Add the tomatoes, water, or stock, and the potatoes. Bring to a boil, then cook over medium heat for 8 to 10 minutes until the potatoes are tender.

Blitz the soup in several batches in a blender for 2 minutes, then pass it through a chinois or fine strainer into a clean pan. Season with salt and pepper to taste.

Warm the poached eggs in boiling water for a few seconds, then drain. Put one in the middle of each warm soup bowl and pour the soup around the eggs. Scatter the reserved lettuce and tomato over the surface and serve at once.

poached eggs on onion tartlets

serves 4

2 large onions, about 1lb 2oz (500g) total weight
8 tbsp (100g) butter
$^2/_3$ cup (150ml) heavy cream
few thyme leaves, plus sprigs to garnish
salt and freshly cracked pepper
$^3/_4$lb (350g) ready-made puff pastry, or tart pie dough (see page 194)
flour, to dust
4 small eggs, poached (see page 44)

Cut the onions into thin slices. Melt the butter in a heavy pan over low heat. Add the onions and cook gently for 45 minutes, stirring every 10 minutes. Pour in the cream, add the thyme leaves, and let simmer for another 20 minutes or so. Season with salt and pepper and tip into a bowl; set aside.

To bake the tartlets, preheat the oven to 325°F (170°C). Roll out the dough on a floured surface to a $^1/_8$ inch (3mm) thickness. Using a $4^1/_2$-inch (12-cm) plain round pastry cutter, cut out 4 disks and place on a baking sheet. Chill for 20 minutes.

Prick each pastry disk 4 or 5 times with a fork. Spread the onions evenly on top of the disks, then bake for 25 to 30 minutes; the bottom of the pastry should be well cooked and crisp.

Put the poached eggs in a bowl, carefully pour on boiling water, and leave them for 30 seconds only to warm through. Drain well and put a poached egg on each onion tartlet. Top with a sprig of thyme and serve on warm plates.

"I sometimes add a little fresh goat cheese to the cream and onions, which makes them even more delicious."

fried eggs

To fry eggs to perfection, all that is needed is to brush the pan with a thin film of melted or softened butter. I cannot abide fried eggs swimming in butter or oil; they aren't at all healthy and I find them totally indigestible. Follow my healthier technique for classic fried eggs (see page 62) unless you prefer a crunchy fried egg, in which case I suggest you try my method for deep-frying eggs (see page 78). "Oeufs sur le plat" are another variation on the fried egg theme. For these, the eggs are cooked in buttered heatproof dishes over indirect heat (see page 70). For me, the perfect partner for fried eggs is ham or bacon, as in the classic ham & eggs (see page 65). The very thought of fried eggs on steak burgers (see page 69) makes my mouth water, and as for "oeufs sur le plat" with morels (see page 77), they are irresistible.

fried eggs

Eggs for frying should always be very fresh. Use a good-quality nonstick skillet for cooking.

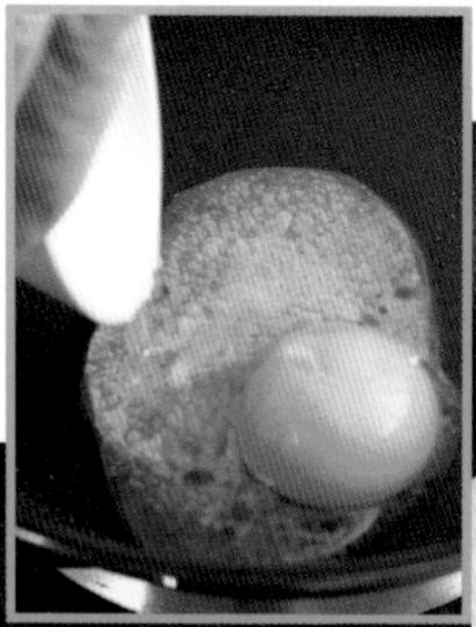

Heat a nonstick skillet until just warm, then brush with softened butter. When the butter is hot, add the eggs one at a time. It is best to break the egg into a ramekin or small bowl first, then slide it into the pan.

When the eggs are done as you like them, take them out of the pan with a spatula. Season with salt and pepper just before serving.

If you like your eggs as well cooked on the top as on the bottom, cover the pan for 30 seconds or up to 1 minute. I prefer this method to turning them over with a spatula, as there is less risk of piercing or breaking the yolks.

ham & eggs

serves 2

2 tbsp (30 g) butter
2 small slices of cooked ham, cut off the bone if possible
2 eggs
salt and freshly ground pepper

In a nonstick skillet, melt the butter over low heat. Put in the ham and turn the slices over after 1 minute, just long enough to warm them through.

Break an egg into a ramekin and slide it gently onto a slice of ham, then repeat with the other egg. Cook gently until the fried eggs are done as you like them (see page 62).

Slide a spatula under each slice of ham and place the ham and eggs on a plate. Season lightly with salt and pepper.

"The secret of good ham and eggs is top quality ham and a very gentle heat. This classic dish is so often ruined by overcooking the ham."

fried quail's eggs on toast with mustard hollandaise

serves 6

2 slices of white bread
4½tbsp (60g) softened butter
1 tsp white wine vinegar
2 tbsp peanut oil
salt and freshly ground pepper
2¼oz (60g) corn salad, trimmed and washed
6 quail's eggs
⅓ cup (100g) mustard hollandaise (page 281)

Cut out 6 circles from the bread with a 1½-inch (4-cm) pastry cutter. Toast under the broiler, then brush on one side with half of the softened butter; keep warm.

Mix the wine vinegar and oil with a little salt and pepper, and toss the corn salad in this dressing.

Brush a warm nonstick skillet with the rest of the softened butter, heat the pan, and fry the quail's eggs (see page 62), allowing 1½ to 2 minutes. Remove from the pan and trim to neaten, using a 1½-inch (4-cm) plain pastry cutter.

Put a toast circle on each warm plate, buttered side-up, and place a fried quail's egg on top. Partially coat the eggs with the mustard hollandaise and put another spoonful of sauce on one side of the plate. Arrange the corn salad on the other side. Serve immediately, as an appetizer.

"I serve this dish with French fries or mousseline potatoes and green beans or a green salad. To fully appreciate the flavor of the meat, it's best not to serve condiments or a sauce—but that's up to you..."

fried eggs on steak burgers

serves 4

1 lb 5 oz (600g) beef steak (preferably round), trimmed of all sinews and fat
salt and freshly ground pepper
$^{1}/_{4}$ cup (60ml) peanut oil
4 medium eggs
softened butter, to fry

Grind the beef through the fine grill of a grinder or, better still, chop it with a knife as finely as possible. Season with salt and pepper. Place a $3^{1}/_{4}$-inch (8-cm) plain pastry cutter on a piece of plastic wrap and put one-quarter of the meat in the middle. Flatten it with the back of a spoon, then carefully lift off the cutter. Repeat to make another 3 steak burgers.

Heat the oil in a skillet or stovetop grill pan. Put in the burgers and fry over high heat for 1 to 2 minutes on each side to seal them, then lower the heat and cook until done to your liking. A rare burger will take 3 to 4 minutes; cook for another 2 to 3 minutes for medium.

At the same time, fry the eggs in a buttered nonstick skillet until cooked to your liking (see page 62). Trim to neat circles, using a 2-inch (5-cm) plain pastry cutter.

Using a spatula, carefully place a fried egg on each steak burger. Transfer to the plates and serve at once.

oeufs sur le plat

Lightly brush the inside of a heatproof egg dish with softened butter.

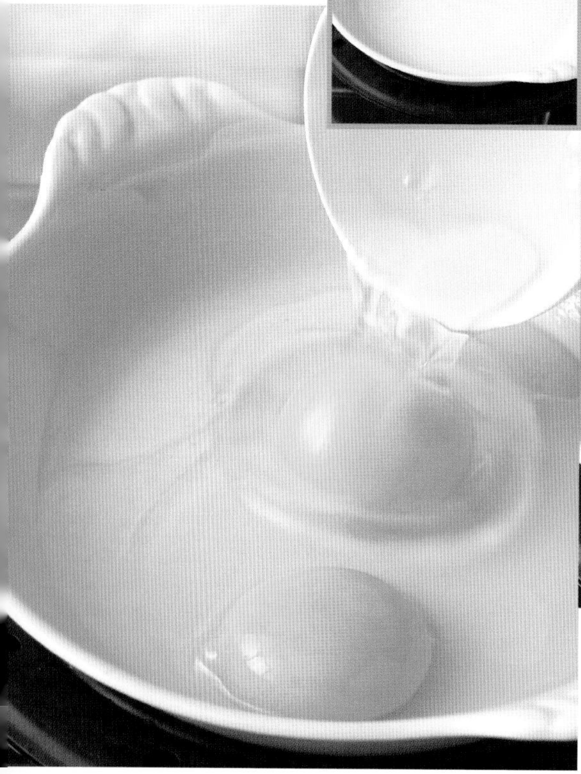

Cook the eggs for 3 to 4 minutes until done as you like them. If you like, place under a hot broiler for 20 seconds to cook the yolks a touch more. Serve in the dish.

Place the dish over indirect heat (using a heat diffuser) and put in 1 or 2 eggs, depending on the size of the dish. I recommend breaking the eggs into a ramekin or small bowl first, then sliding them into the dish.

"oeufs sur le plat" with parsley beurre blanc

serves 4

8 eggs
$4^1/_2$tbsp (60g) softened butter, to grease
for the parsley beurre blanc
1oz (30g) shallots, chopped
$^2/_3$ cup (150ml) dry white wine
1tbsp heavy cream
$4^1/_2$tbsp (60g) butter, diced
2tbsp snipped Italian parsley leaves
salt and freshly ground pepper

First make the beurre blanc. Put the chopped shallots in a small pan and add the white wine. Bring to a boil and reduce over medium heat by two-thirds. Add the cream and let bubble for a few moments. Whisk in the diced butter, then take the pan off the heat and add the snipped parsley. Season with salt and pepper; keep warm.

Brush 4 egg dishes with softened butter. Break 2 eggs, one at a time, into a ramekin, and slide them into one dish. Repeat with the other 6 eggs. Cook the eggs to your liking (see left).

Spoon the parsley beurre blanc over the eggs and serve immediately.

"This delectable butter sauce is the ideal complement to *oeufs sur le plat*. Its slight acidity counteracts the richness of the egg yolks and enhances the flavor."

"oeufs sur le plat" with sorrel & tomato coulis

serves 2

12 small, tender sorrel leaves
2 tbsp (30g) softened butter
4 eggs
for the tomato coulis
1 large, very ripe tomato, skinned, seeded, and diced
2½ tbsp olive oil
1 small garlic clove, chopped
1 thyme sprig
salt and freshly ground pepper

First make the tomato coulis. Put the tomato, olive oil, garlic, and thyme in a small pan and cook over low heat for about 10 seconds, until the tomato is softened. Immediately discard the thyme and blitz the tomato in a blender for a few seconds. Season with salt and pepper; keep warm.

Cut two of the sorrel leaves into fine julienne and keep for the garnish.

Brush the bottom of 2 egg dishes with the softened butter. Arrange the rest of the sorrel in the egg dishes and set them on a heat diffuser over medium heat until the sorrel begins to wilt. Immediately break 2 eggs into a ramekin and slide them onto the sorrel in one dish. Repeat with the other 2 eggs. Cook until done to your liking (see page 70).

Serve the eggs in their dishes. Scatter over the sorrel julienne and pour the tomato coulis around the edge. Serve at once.

"This dish is a delight. The sorrel adds a touch of acidity, contrasting with the mellowness of the egg, and the natural freshness of the tomato gives it a lift."

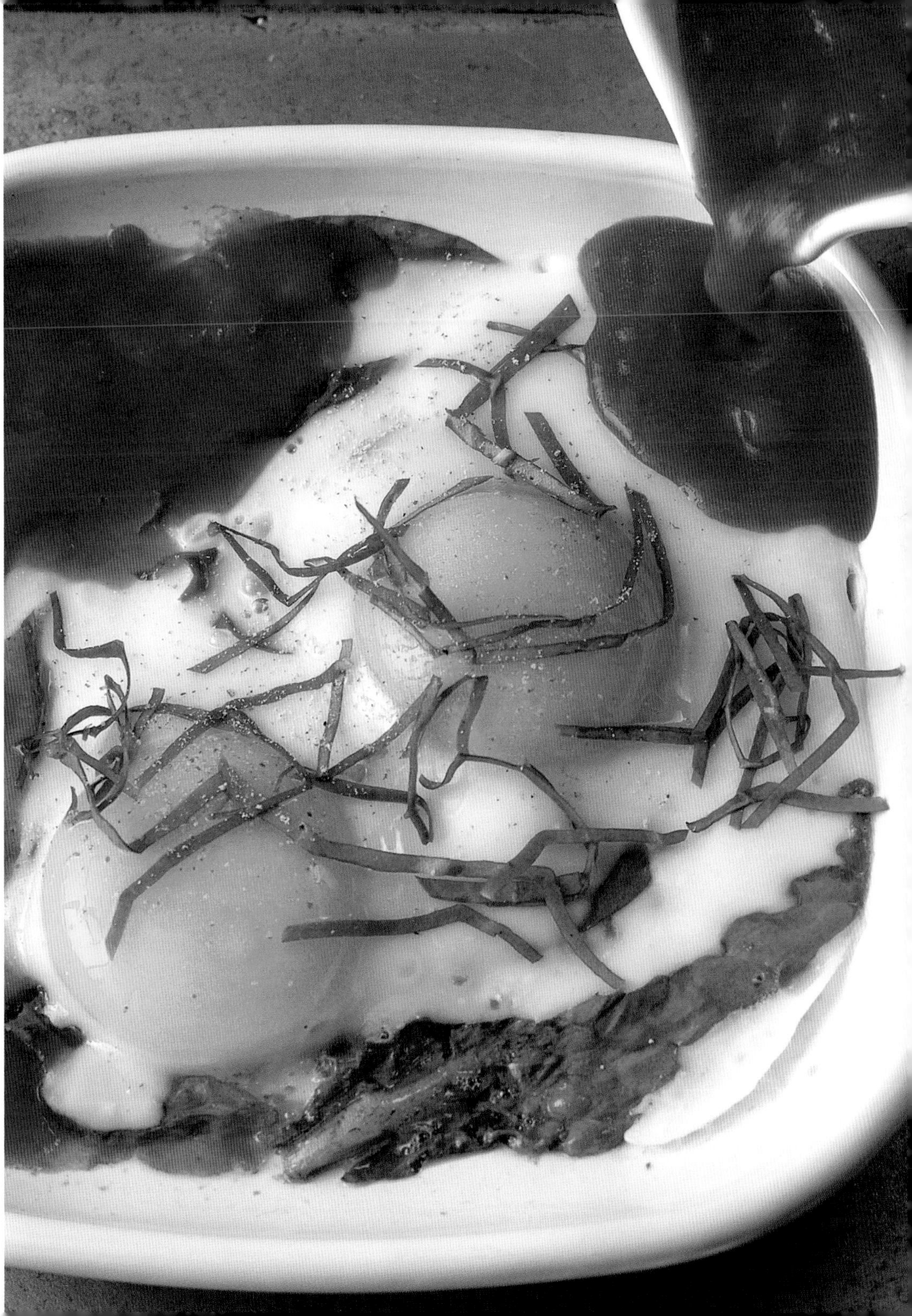

"oeufs sur le plat" with asparagus tips & coulis

serves 4

"Asparagus is the perfect partner for an egg."

24 small asparagus spears
salt and freshly ground pepper
3 tbsp (40g) butter, plus 4½ tbsp (60g) softened butter to grease dishes
1 shallot, finely chopped
8 eggs
1 tbsp snipped Italian parsley leaves

Thinly peel the lower part of the asparagus stalks. Cut off the tips leaving 1¼-inch (3-cm) stalk attached. Dice the lower part of the stalks. Cook the asparagus tips in boiling salted water for 1 to 2 minutes, depending on whether you like them crunchy or just firm. Refresh in cold water and drain.

To make the coulis, melt 3 tbsp (40g) butter in a small pan. Add the shallot and diced asparagus stalks, cover, and sweat very gently for 3 minutes. Add a generous ⅓ cup (100 ml) water and cook, uncovered, over medium heat for 5 minutes. Purée in a blender, then pass through a chinois or fine strainer into a small pan. If the coulis is not thick enough, reduce it over low heat for a few minutes, until it lightly coats the back of a spoon. Season to taste and keep hot.

Brush 4 egg dishes with butter. Arrange 6 asparagus tips at the edge of each dish. Break 2 eggs, one at a time, into a ramekin, and slide into a dish. Repeat with the other dishes. Cook to your liking (see page 70).

Put a dish on each plate and pour a little coulis over the asparagus tips. Sprinkle with the parsley, and serve the rest of the coulis separately.

"oeufs sur le plat" with morels

serves 4

"The flavor of this dish is absolutely divine when it is made with fresh morels in season. It's the perfect appetizer for a special lunch."

14oz (400g) fresh morels, or 4oz (100g) dried
4½tbsp (60g) butter
1 shallot, finely chopped
2 tbsp heavy cream
salt and freshly ground pepper
4½tbsp (60g) softened butter
8 eggs
1 tbsp snipped chervil leaves

Pare the fresh morels with a small sharp knife, cut off the bottom of the stalks, and halve larger morels lengthwise. Rinse in cold water to eliminate all traces of sand or grit, and drain well. If you are using dried mushrooms, put them in a large bowl and cover with plenty of boiling water. Leave for 2 hours, then drain.

Heat 4½tbsp (60g) butter in a skillet set over medium heat and add the morels. Fresh morels will cook in 4 to 6 minutes; allow 3 to 4 for dried. Add the shallot and cook gently for 1 minute. Stir in the cream and cook for another 30 seconds. Season with salt and pepper to taste. Keep warm.

Lightly brush the inside of 4 egg dishes with softened butter. Break 2 eggs, one at a time, into a ramekin, and slide them into a dish. Repeat with the other 6 eggs. Cook to your liking (see page 70).

Put 2 fried eggs on each plate. Divide the morels between the plates, arranging them around the eggs. Sprinkle the snipped chervil over the eggs and serve immediately.

crunchy fried eggs

Two-thirds fill a small, heavy pan with peanut oil and heat over medium heat to 350°F (180°C).

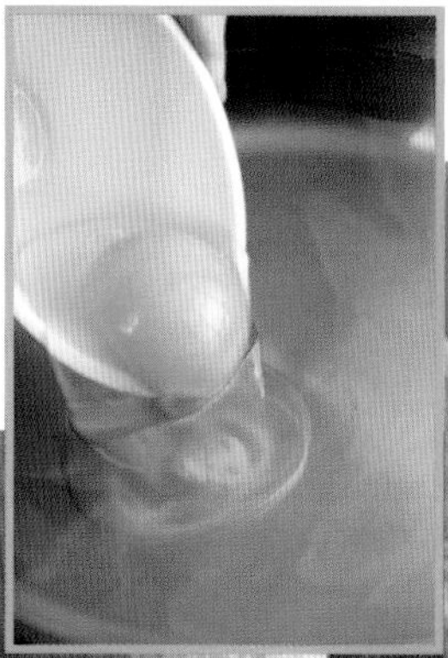

Break an egg into a ramekin or small bowl and gently slide it into the hot oil.

After a few seconds, the egg will begin to fry. Use two wooden spatulas or spoons to lift any egg white that has spread out back over the egg to maintain a rounded shape.

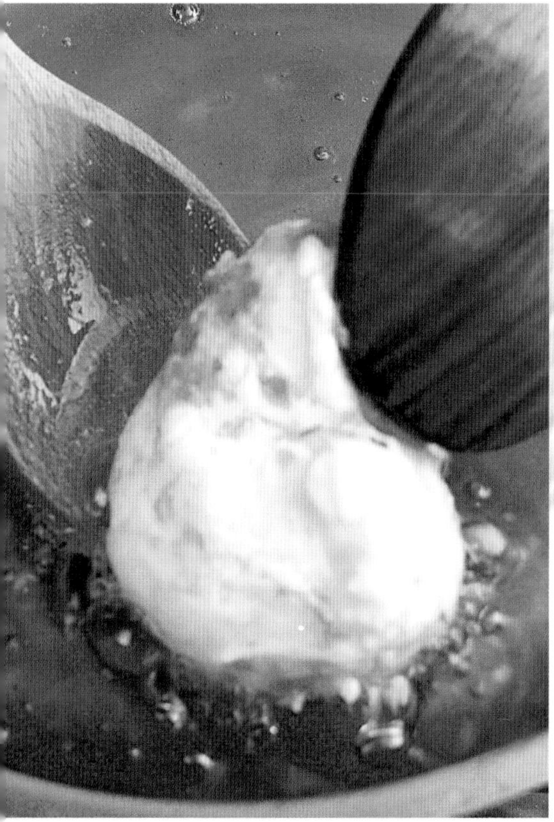

After $1\frac{1}{2}$ to 2 minutes, the egg will be crunchy on the outside and the yolk will still be slightly runny. Lift it out of the oil with a slotted spoon and drain on paper towels.

After 1 minute, carefully turn the egg over in the oil so that it cooks evenly.

The sooner you serve the egg, the better it will be. It is best to fry the eggs individually, but you can cook two at a time if you do it very carefully.

crunchy fried eggs in a nest of broiled eggplants

serves 4

2 long eggplants, about 9oz (250g) each
1/4 cup (50ml) olive oil
salt
peanut oil, to deep-fry
4 large eggs
3/4oz (20g) curly parsley leaves, washed and well dried

With a very sharp knife, cut the eggplants lengthwise into 1/8-inch (4–5-mm) thick slices, discarding the outer slices. Place the eggplant slices in a dish, brush with the olive oil, and salt lightly.

Heat a stovetop grill pan or griddle until very hot. Add 3 or 4 eggplant slices and cook for 1 minute, then give them a quarter-turn and cook for another minute to mark a grid lattice pattern. Turn the slices over and repeat on the other side. Put them in a dish lined with waxed paper and keep warm.

Heat the peanut oil in a heavy, deep pan and deep-fry the eggs to your liking (see page 78). Drain on paper towels.

Lower the temperature of the oil slightly to 315°F (160°C), drop in the parsley, stir with a slotted spoon, and deep-fry for 1 minute until very crisp. Remove with the spoon and drain on paper towels.

Arrange the eggplant slices like little nests on 4 plates. Put a fried egg in each cavity and scatter with fried parsley. Serve immediately.

crunchy fried eggs on darphin potatoes with spinach

serves 4

9oz (250g) potatoes, Russet or round white
salt and freshly ground pepper
8 tbsp peanut oil, plus extra to deep-fry
1 tbsp red wine vinegar
4 eggs
$1\frac{1}{2}$oz (40g) baby spinach, washed and drained

Peel the potatoes, then cut into fine julienne on a mandolin. Place in a bowl, without rinsing so that the starch is retained. Salt lightly and leave for 3 to 4 minutes.

Combine 3 tbsp oil, the wine vinegar, and a little salt and pepper in a bowl to make a vinaigrette.

To make the Darphin potatoes, use 4 small skillets, about 4 inches (10 cm) in diameter if you have them; otherwise, use one large pan. Heat 5 tbsp oil in the pan(s). Squeeze the potatoes in a cloth to dry. Put them into the pan(s) and flatten into uniform cake(s), pressing them with a spatula. Cook over medium heat for 3 to 4 minutes, until golden brown, then turn them over with the spatula and cook the other side for 3 to 4 minutes. Drain on paper towels.

Heat the oil for deep-frying in a suitable pan and cook the eggs to your liking (see page 78). Drain on paper towels.

Delicately mix the spinach leaves into the vinaigrette. If you've made a single, large Darphin, cut into portions with scissors. Put a potato cake on each plate and top with a fried egg. Arrange the dressed spinach around the eggs and the potatoes. Serve a pear chutney or salsa on the side if you like.

crunchy fried eggs on dandelion salad

serves 4

14oz (400g) very tender yellow or green dandelion leaves, trimmed
6tbsp peanut oil, plus extra to deep-fry
2tbsp white wine vinegar
salt and freshly ground pepper
1 large white onion, peeled
generous 1/3 cup (100ml) milk
1/3 cup (50g) all-purpose flour, to dust
pinch of paprika
4 eggs
1oz (30g) shallots, finely chopped

Wash the dandelion leaves in very cold water, drain, and place in the refrigerator. Make a dressing with 6tbsp oil, the wine vinegar, and salt and pepper to taste.

Cut the onion into thin rings and let soak in the milk for 5 minutes, then drain. Season the flour with a pinch of salt and a smidgeon of paprika. Sprinkle the onion rings very lightly with the seasoned flour. Heat a generous 1 cup (200ml) peanut oil in a deep skillet to 350°F (180°C). Drop in the onion rings and deep-fry until just golden and crisp. Drain and set aside on paper towels.

Heat the peanut oil for deep-frying in a heavy, deep pan and cook the eggs to your liking (see page 78). Drain on paper towels.

Mix the dandelion leaves with the dressing and chopped shallots. Divide between 4 plates and place a fried egg in the middle. Scatter some onion rings around and serve at once.

"I adore this. The crisp fried eggs and onions marry perfectly with the dandelion leaves, and transform a classic rustic dandelion salad with bacon into something very special."

scrambled eggs

Scrambling is the finest way to cook eggs in my opinion. My brother, Albert, uses the classic method of cooking them slowly in a bain-marie, but I prefer the quicker, more modern approach of scrambling eggs in a pan over low heat on a heat diffuser. Perfect for breakfast, lunch, or a weekend brunch, they always look inviting, whether you present them on a plate, on toast, or in warm pita bread. For a taste of Mexico, I mix them with snipped herbs, chopped tomatoes, and diced red onions, and serve them cold in tacos. When truffles are in season, simply macerate a few raw truffle peelings or trimmings in the eggs for several hours, then scramble them to make the most perfect dish imaginable. The recipes in this chapter take account of the seasons and they are some of my favorite egg dishes. I encourage you to try them all...

scrambled eggs **serves 2**

Allow 2 medium eggs per person for an appetizer or light snack, or 3 medium eggs per person for a main course.

Cook over low heat, stirring gently and more or less constantly with a wooden spoon.

Melt 3 tbsp (40 g) butter in a shallow, heavy pan set on a heat diffuser over low heat, or in a bain-marie. Break 4–6 eggs into a bowl and beat very lightly with a fork. Tip into the pan with the hot, melted butter and stir.

It will take 3 to 4 minutes for the eggs to become just set, but very creamy. (If using a bain-marie, allow about 6 minutes). If you prefer firmer, dryer scrambled eggs, cook for another 2 minutes.

When the eggs are scrambled to your liking, add 2 tbsp light or heavy cream or a little bit of butter, and season with salt and pepper. Scrambled eggs are best served immediately.

scrambled eggs "magda" on fried bread

serves 2

3 slices of white bread, 1/4 inch (5mm) thick
6 tbsp peanut oil
3 tbsp (40g) butter
4 eggs, beaten
1 tbsp light or heavy cream
salt and freshly ground pepper
1 tbsp strong Dijon mustard
1 tbsp snipped Italian parsley leaves, plus extra leaves to garnish
1 tbsp snipped chives
1 oz (30g) Gruyère, grated

Cut off the crusts from the bread, then cut the slices diagonally in half. Heat the oil in a skillet over medium heat until hot, and fry the bread triangles until golden on both sides. Keep warm on paper towels.

Melt the butter in a heavy pan, add the beaten eggs, and scramble (see page 88). Add the cream at the end of cooking and season with salt and pepper. Stir in the mustard, snipped herbs, and grated Gruyère, and adjust the seasoning.

Put 3 fried bread triangles on each plate, overlapping them slightly. Spoon the scrambled eggs on top, garnish with parsley leaves, and serve immediately.
An ideal winter breakfast.

scrambled eggs in small potatoes with salmon eggs

serves 8

"If you're feeling extravagant, top the potatoes with real caviar only."

32 small new potatoes, about 14oz (400g), preferably round white, washed
salt and freshly ground pepper
6½tbsp (80g) butter
8 eggs, beaten
2tbsp light or heavy cream
1oz (30g) sevruga caviar
1oz (30g) lumpfish roe
2¼oz (60g) salmon eggs

Put the potatoes in a pan, cover with lightly salted cold water, and cook for about 15 minutes. To check if they are cooked, slide in a knife tip; it should meet with no resistance. Turn off the heat and pour a little cold water into the pan to stop the cooking. Let the potatoes cool completely, then drain and pat dry.

Cut off a ¼-inch (5-mm) thick lid with a sharp knife, then using a melon baller or coffee spoon, scoop out the insides of the potatoes, leaving a ¼-inch (5-mm) layer in the skins. Season lightly with salt and pepper, cover with plastic wrap, and set aside.

Melt the butter in a heavy pan, add the beaten eggs, and scramble (see page 88). Add the cream at the end of cooking and season with salt and pepper. Tip the scrambled eggs into a bowl and set over a bowl of cold water with ice cubes added. Keep stirring the eggs every 2 or 3 minutes until the eggs are cold, then remove the bowl from the ice water.

Fill the potatoes generously with scrambled egg and top each one with a little caviar, lumpfish roe, or salmon eggs. Arrange the potatoes on a platter to serve as canapés, or allow 4 per person for an appetizer.

illustrated on previous page

scrambled eggs in smoked salmon papillotes

serves 4

"Serve these papillotes with a lemony cucumber salad for a perfect brunch or lunch."

4 good slices of smoked salmon, about 4½oz (120g) each
½oz (15g) dill
6½oz (80g) butter
8 eggs, beaten
4 tbsp light or heavy cream
salt and freshly ground pepper
1 lemon, cut into quarters

Trim the smoked salmon to make neat rectangles or squares; set aside at room temperature. Finely dice the trimmings and put them in a bowl. Reserve 4 dill sprigs for the garnish, snip the rest, and add to the diced salmon.

Melt the butter in a heavy pan, add the beaten eggs, and scramble (see page 88). Add the cream at the end, then the diced salmon and snipped dill. Season with salt and pepper.

Lay the smoked salmon slices on a sheet of plastic wrap. Put the scrambled eggs in the middle of the slices and fold one side of the salmon over the eggs, then the other to make papillotes. Turn them over.

Using a palette knife, lift each papillote onto a plate. With a very sharp knife, make a 2-inch (5-cm) long incision in the top to reveal some of the egg. Arrange a dill sprig in each slit, put a lemon quarter on each plate, and serve at once.

scrambled eggs with crab & asparagus tips

serves 4

36 small asparagus spears
salt and freshly ground pepper
6½ tbsp (80g) butter
8 eggs, beaten
2 tbsp light or heavy cream
8 cooked shelled crab claws, or 5½ oz (160g) cooked white crabmeat
1 tsp (5g) chives, cut into short lengths

Peel the asparagus stalks thinly with a vegetable peeler and cut off the tips leaving about 1½-inch (4-cm) stalk attached to them. Cook in boiling salted water for 2 to 3 minutes; the asparagus should be firm but not crunchy. Refresh in cold water and keep at room temperature.

Melt the butter in a heavy pan, add the beaten eggs, and scramble (see page 88). Add the cream at the end of cooking and season with salt and pepper.

Steam the crabmeat or shelled claws for 2 to 3 minutes to heat them, then add the asparagus and steam for another minute, until just hot.

Divide the scrambled eggs between 4 plates. Place 2 crab claws or a pile of crabmeat in the center, arrange the asparagus tips around the crab, scatter with the chives, and serve at once.

"For optimum flavor, use the meat from a freshly cooked live crab. My clients love this dish; it's a great favorite of my friend Egon Ronay."

scrambled eggs clamart

serves 4

12 small snow peas
1 cup (100g) shelled fresh or frozen peas
$\frac{1}{2}$ lettuce, or 6–8 outer lettuce leaves
8 tbsp (100g) butter
8 eggs, beaten
2 tbsp light or heavy cream
salt and freshly ground pepper

Slice the snow peas on the diagonal, then cook briefly in boiling water; they should still be crunchy. Drain, refresh in cold water, and set aside. Cook the peas briefly in boiling water until barely tender; drain, refresh, and set aside.

Wash the lettuce leaves in cold water, drain well, and snip finely into shreds. Place in a pan with $1\frac{1}{2}$ tbsp (20g) butter and sweat gently for 1 to 2 minutes; keep warm.

Melt the remaining $6\frac{1}{2}$ tbsp (80g) butter in a heavy pan, add the beaten eggs, and scramble (see page 88). Add the cream at the end of cooking and season with salt and pepper.

Heat the peas and snow peas in boiling water for 20 seconds, then drain. Mix the peas and lettuce into the scrambled eggs. Divide between 4 plates and arrange the snow peas in the middle. Serve at once.

"The vegetables add a touch of sweetness to this delicate, fresh dish, which makes a lovely appetizer in spring or early summer, when the first fresh peas and snow peas appear in the market. Use an outdoor-grown lettuce if possible."

scrambled eggs with rhubarb

serves 4

"This dish, which I created a good twenty years ago, still makes an occasional appearance on the Waterside Inn menu. The acidity of the rhubarb contrasts perfectly with the egg."

7oz (200g) very tender young rhubarb
½ cup (100g) sugar
2 slices of white bread, ½ inch (1cm) thick
8 tbsp peanut oil
6½ tbsp (80g) butter
8 eggs, beaten
4 tbsp light or heavy cream
salt and freshly ground pepper

Peel the rhubarb if it is slightly stringy, wash in cold water, and drain. Finely dice two-thirds of the rhubarb and cut the rest into small or large sticks.

Dissolve the sugar in a generous ⅓ cup (100 ml) water in a pan over low heat, then bring to a boil. Add the diced rhubarb and cook for 30 seconds, then remove with a slotted spoon and place in a bowl; keep warm. Bring the syrup back to a boil, add the rhubarb sticks, and cook for 45 seconds to 1 minute, until just firm. Drain and set aside.

Cut off the crusts from the bread and cut the slices into large cubes. Heat the oil in a skillet and fry the bread cubes over medium heat until golden all over. Drain the croutons on paper towels.

Melt the butter in a heavy pan, add the beaten eggs, and scramble (see page 88). Add the cream at the end of cooking, then the diced rhubarb. Season.

Divide the scrambled eggs between 4 plates and scatter over the rhubarb sticks and the croutons. Serve immediately.

portuguese-style scrambled eggs

serves 4

4 small clusters of cherry tomatoes (5–6 on each stalk)
$^1/_4$ cup (50ml) olive oil
1 garlic clove, crushed
salt and freshly ground pepper
$6^1/_2$tbsp (80g) butter
8 eggs, beaten
2tbsp light or heavy cream
pan juices from roast chicken, lamb, or pork, skimmed of fat
12 Italian parsley leaves, to garnish

Soak the clusters of cherry tomatoes in cold water for 20 minutes. Preheat the oven to 212°F (100°C). Mix the olive oil with the garlic. Drain the tomato clusters and brush them generously with garlicky oil. Sprinkle with a little salt, place on a rack set over a roasting pan, and cook in the oven for 20 minutes.

Melt the butter in a heavy pan, add the beaten eggs, and scramble (see page 88). Add the cream at the end of cooking and season with salt and pepper.

Divide the scrambled eggs between 4 deep plates. Put a cluster of cherry tomatoes in the middle of each portion and pour a ribbon of warm chicken or meat juices around the eggs. Garnish with parsley leaves and serve immediately.

"Pan juices from a roast add a wonderful complexity to the scrambled eggs in this rich dish, which is nonetheless refreshing, thanks to the tomatoes. It is perfect for a light lunch."

scrambled eggs masala

serves 2

4 eggs
2 tbsp (30ml) milk
1 tbsp finely chopped cilantro
salt
2 tbsp (30g) butter
2 tbsp (30ml) peanut oil
1 red onion, about 5oz (150g), finely chopped
1 small green chile
pinch of ground red pimiento
5oz (150g) tomatoes, skinned, seeded, and diced

Break the eggs into a bowl, whisk in the milk and chopped cilantro, and season lightly with salt.

Heat the butter and oil preferably in a wok, or a nonstick skillet. Add the onion and sweat gently until it turns pink. Meanwhile, halve and seed the chile, remove the white membrane, then finely dice the flesh. Add to the onion with the pimiento and tomatoes, and cook for 3 to 4 minutes.

Pour the beaten eggs into the wok or pan, stirring with a spoon, and scramble lightly for about 1 minute, until soft and creamy.

Serve the scrambled eggs on warm plates, accompanied with warm croissants or flaky parathas.

"My friend Rasoi Vineet Bhatia cooks these scrambled eggs exquisitely. I love to serve them while on vacation in Provence, under the summer skies. They bring India to my door and introduce a feeling of serenity."

baked eggs

Baked eggs "en cocotte" are deliciously delicate. They can be prepared in advance and kept in their ramekins in the refrigerator, ready to cook in a bain-marie just a few minutes before serving. I adore all the recipes in this chapter, but my favorite is truffled eggs en cocotte (see page 111). Nicole, the wife of my dear pâtissier friend, Frédéric Jouvaud from Carpentras, always makes this dish for me when I visit them during the truffle season. Naturally, the truffles come from nearby Mont Ventoux. To impart flavor, Nicole puts a few truffles in an airtight box with the eggs a day before my arrival. When she breaks the eggs into the ramekins, they release the most wonderful aroma. It is agonizing waiting while the eggs are baking in the oven! I particularly love to prepare this recipe for a celebration, such as New Year's Eve dinner.

baked eggs

Bring the eggs to room temperature. Preheat the oven to 325°F (170°C).

Brush the insides of the ramekins or cocottes with softened butter, stopping 1/2 inch (1 cm) below the rim. Season the dish lightly with salt and pepper.

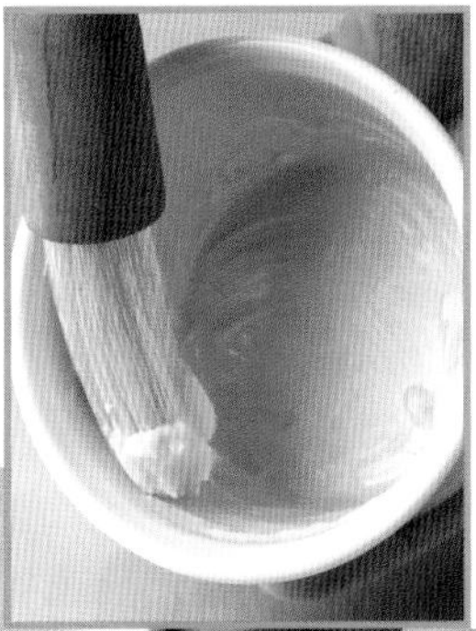

Carefully break an egg into a small dish and tip it gently into the ramekin. Repeat with the rest.

Drizzle a little heavy cream (about 1 tbsp) onto each egg white, taking care that none runs onto the yolk.

Line a shallow roasting pan with waxed paper. Put in the ramekins and gently pour boiling water around them to come halfway up the molds. Place in the oven.

Check the baked eggs after 10 minutes; the egg white should be just set but the yolk should still be runny. If you prefer your egg a little more cooked, bake for another 2 or 3 minutes.

truffled eggs en cocotte

serves 4

"This is a great favorite at The Waterside Inn, where it features on the menu when fresh truffles are in season—from December to February."

4 eggs
$2^1/_4$oz (60g) fresh black truffles
6 tbsp heavy cream
2 tbsp (30g) softened butter
salt and freshly ground pepper
$2^1/_4$oz (60g) Emmental or Comté, grated

Put the eggs in an airtight container with the truffles and keep in the refrigerator for at least 24 hours, or 48 hours if possible to allow the aroma of the truffles to permeate the eggs.

Slice the truffles as thinly as possible. Bring the cream to a boil in a small pan, then immediately drop in the truffles and turn off the heat. Stir the truffles into the cream with a spoon, cover the pan, and set aside until almost cold.

Preheat the oven to 325°F (170°C). Brush the insides of 4 cocottes or ramekins, about $3^1/_4$ inches (8cm) in diameter and $1^1/_2$ inches (4 cm) deep, with the softened butter and season with salt and pepper. Put three-quarters of the grated cheese into one cocotte and rotate it to coat the inside. Tip the excess cheese into a second cocotte and repeat to coat all 4 dishes.

Divide the cooled cream and truffle mixture between the cocottes. Carefully tip an egg into each one, sprinkle on the remaining cheese, and bake the eggs (see page 109) until cooked to your liking.

Put a cocotte on each plate and serve.

baked eggs with chicken livers & shallots in wine

serves 4

scant 1 cup (200ml) red wine, such as Pinot noir
1 thyme sprig
1 bay leaf
1 shallot, finely sliced
1/4 cup veal stock, or 1/3 cup chicken stock
2 chicken livers, trimmed of sinews
1 tbsp peanut oil
salt and freshly ground pepper
2 tbsp (30g) softened butter
4 eggs

Preheat the oven to 325°F (170°C). Put the wine, thyme, and bay leaf in a small pan and reduce by half over low heat. Add the shallot and veal or chicken stock, and reduce until thick enough to generously coat the back of a spoon. Discard the thyme and bay leaf and set aside the shallot in wine.

Cut the chicken livers into small pieces. Heat the oil in a small skillet and quickly sear the livers for 30 seconds. Season, put into a bowl, and set aside.

Brush the insides of 4 cocottes or ramekins, about 3 1/4 inches (8cm) in diameter and 1 1/2 inches (4 cm) deep, with the softened butter and season lightly with salt and pepper. Mix the chicken livers with the wine and shallots, season to taste, and divide between the cocottes. Carefully tip an egg into each one and bake the eggs (see page 109) until cooked to your liking.

Put a cocotte on each plate and serve immediately, with small slices of toasted country-style bread.

baked eggs with smoked ham & toasted hazelnuts

serves 4

"Smoked ham and eggs are in perfect harmony here, and the toasted nuts add a contrasting texture and flavor. Serve with toast."

2 tbsp (30g) softened butter
salt and freshly ground pepper
4 eggs
3 1/4oz (80g) lightly smoked ham, diced
4 tbsp heavy cream
8 freshly toasted skinned hazelnuts, halved

Preheat the oven to 325°F (170°C). Take 4 cocotte molds, preferably glass, about 2 1/2 inches (6cm) in diameter and 2 1/2 inches (6cm) deep, and brush with softened butter. Season lightly with salt and pepper.

Carefully tip an egg into each mold, then scatter the diced ham and spoon the cream over the egg whites. Bake the eggs (see page 109) until cooked to your liking.

Put a cocotte on each plate. Arrange 4 toasted hazelnut halves around each egg yolk and serve immediately.

illustrated on previous page

baked eggs with smoked haddock & grain mustard

serves 4

about 4½oz (120g) lightly smoked haddock
1¼ cups (300ml) milk
6 tbsp heavy cream
1 tbsp Meaux or grain mustard
salt and freshly ground pepper
2 tbsp (30g) softened butter
4 eggs
1 tbsp snipped Italian parsley leaves

Put the haddock and milk in a small pan, bring to a boil over low heat, and then immediately take the pan off the heat. Let the haddock cool slowly in the milk; it will finish cooking as it does so.

Preheat the oven to 325°F (170°C). Drain the smoked haddock, remove the skin, and flake the flesh. Heat the cream in a small pan. As soon as it comes to a boil, add the flaked haddock, and take the pan off the heat. Stir in the mustard and season to taste. Keep at room temperature.

Brush the insides of 4 cocottes or ramekins, about 3¼ inches (8 cm) in diameter and 1½ inches (4 cm) deep, with softened butter, then season lightly with salt and pepper. Divide the haddock and cream mixture between the cocottes. Carefully tip an egg into each one and bake (see page 109) until cooked to your liking.

Put a cocotte on each plate, sprinkle with snipped parsley, and serve immediately.

"It's impossible to resist these little shrimp, which are divine with the eggs and cream, and perhaps a slice of toast on the side. One egg is enough for an appetizer, but I would serve two for a lunch or light main course."

baked eggs with shrimp & capers

serves 4

48 cooked small shrimp or 28 large shrimp in the shell
2 tbsp (30g) softened butter
salt and freshly ground pepper
4 eggs
4 tbsp heavy cream
24 small capers, rinsed and well drained

Preheat the oven to 325°F (170°C). Shell the shrimp, leaving eight with their heads attached for the garnish.

Take 4 cocotte molds about 3¼ inches (8cm) in diameter and 1½ inches (4cm) deep, and brush with the softened butter. Season lightly with salt and pepper. Carefully tip an egg into each mold, drizzle the cream over the egg whites, then scatter the shelled shrimp and capers over the yolks. Bake the eggs (see page 109) until cooked to your liking.

Serve immediately, garnished with the whole shrimp.

eggs en cocotte with girolles

serves 4

"If girolles are not available, use cèpes, black trumpets, or white mushrooms instead. This dish is perfect as an appetizer, but if you want to serve it as a main course, allow 2 eggs per person."

about 4½oz (125g) girolles
1½tbsp softened butter, plus 2tbsp to grease
scant 1 cup (200ml) heavy cream
juice of ½ lemon
2tsp snipped Italian parsley leaves
leaves from 1 small thyme sprig
salt and freshly ground pepper
4 eggs

Preheat the oven to 325°F (170°C). Clean the girolles, scraping off any earth or sand with a small knife, then wipe gently with a slightly damp cloth. Cut 4 thin slices from the middle of the best girolles and set aside. Finely chop the rest.

Heat a little bit of butter in a small skillet and sauté the mushroom slices for 30 seconds on each side until golden; set aside for the garnish.

Pour two-thirds of the cream into a pan and boil over medium heat until reduced by one-quarter. Add the chopped girolles and lemon juice, and cook gently for about 5 minutes. Take off the heat, add the parsley and thyme, season to taste, and let cool.

Brush the insides of 4 cocottes or ramekins, about 3¼ inches (8cm) in diameter and 1½ inches (4cm) deep with softened butter and season. Divide the cream and girolle mixture between the dishes. Carefully tip an egg into each one and pour the rest of the cream over the whites. Bake (see page 109) until cooked to your liking.

Place a cocotte on each plate and put a sautéed girolle slice on top of each egg. Serve immediately, with fingers of hot toast for dipping into the yolks.

french toast "eiderdown" with herbs & bacon

serves 8

8 lean bacon slices, derinded
3 tbsp (40g) softened butter
8–10 medium-thick slices of good-quality white bread
3 tbsp snipped chives
3 tbsp snipped Italian parsley leaves
3 tbsp snipped chervil
1 tbsp snipped tarragon
4 scallions, finely snipped
3oz (75g) Emmental, grated
3oz (75g) Cheddar, grated
1oz (30g) Parmesan, grated, plus 3 tbsp to finish
salt and freshly ground pepper
8 eggs
800ml milk

Fry the bacon briefly in a dry skillet until golden brown, no more than 1½ minutes. Cut into 2-inch (5-cm) pieces and set aside on a plate.

Brush a rectangular ovenproof dish, about 10½ x 7 x 2½ inches (26 x 18 x 6 cm), with the softened butter. Remove the crusts from the bread and cut each slice into 3 wide strips. Mix together the herbs and scallions. Combine the grated cheeses.

Cover the bottom of the dish with a layer of bread, season with salt and pepper, and scatter over some of the herb mixture. Sprinkle with a layer of grated cheese, and finally a sprinkling of bacon. Repeat these layers, then finish with a layer of bread; it should be about ½ inch (1 cm) below the rim of the dish.

Beat the eggs with the milk and seasoning. Pour over the bread, sprinkle with Parmesan, and cover with plastic wrap. Leave in the refrigerator for 24 hours or, better still, 48 hours.

To cook, preheat the oven to 325°F (170°C). Bake the dish for about 45 minutes, until the mixture has risen 1¼–1½ inches (3–4 cm) above the rim and is golden. Check the cooking by inserting a knife tip into the center; it should come out clean. Serve from the oven, while still soft in the middle. A great favorite with children.

FONTINA

little parmesan & fontina flans

serves 6

2 eggs
generous $^1/_3$ cup (100ml) light cream
scant 1 cup (200ml) heavy cream
4oz (100g) fontina, grated
1oz (30g) Parmesan, grated
salt and freshly ground pepper
pinch of freshly grated nutmeg
$1^1/_2$tbsp (20g) softened butter

Break the eggs into a large bowl, beat them with a fork as for an omelet, then add the light and heavy creams and beat until smooth. Mix in the cheeses and season with very little salt and as much pepper as you wish.

Preheat the oven to 315°F (160°C). Brush the insides of 6 cocottes or ramekins, about $3^1/_4$ inches (8cm) in diameter and $1^1/_2$ inches (4cm) deep, with softened butter and season with salt and pepper. Divide the egg mixture between the cocottes.

Stand the dishes in a shallow ovenproof dish lined with waxed paper. Pour in just enough boiling water to come halfway up the sides of the cocottes, then place in the oven. Check the cooking after 15 to 20 minutes; the little flans should be just set at the edge and slightly trembling in the middle. Take the cocottes out of the bain-marie and let cool on a wire rack.

Serve the flans in the cocottes on plates. They are best served cold, but not chilled.

"For a brunch or summer buffet, bake one flan in a large gratin dish, allowing an extra 15 minutes in the oven; serve with a salad."

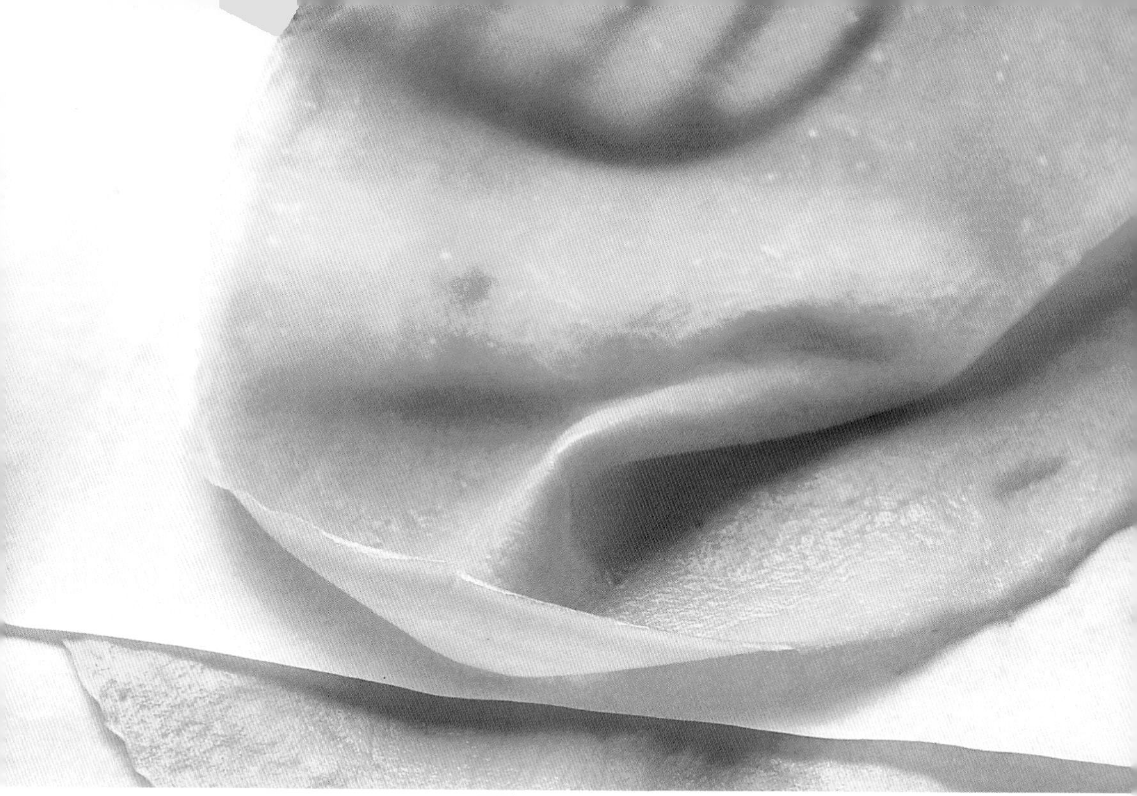

omelets

Omelets are quick to prepare, simple to cook, easy to digest, and perfect for a one-dish meal. The great food writer Elizabeth David often spoke about her passion for omelets when she ate at Le Gavroche. Her book "An Omelette and a Glass of Wine" is testimony to her love of omelets and I was flattered to be asked to write a foreword. Depending on taste, an omelet can be well cooked, moist, or runny in the middle (*baveuse*), which is how I like it. In my view, the color should be very light golden; some prefer a deeper shade and others like their omelets very pale, which I call anemic. You can also make an omelet using only egg whites. My favorite definition of the perfect omelet (from Mlle Cécile de Rothschild) is well rounded, with just a touch of color; delicate to touch, squidgy, and soft "as a baby's bottom."

omelets

serves 2

Allow 2 eggs per person for an appetizer or light snack; allow 3 eggs per person for a main course.

Break the eggs into a bowl, season with salt and pepper, and beat lightly with a fork. Heat an 8-inch (20-cm) skillet, preferably nonstick. When the pan is hot, quickly brush a little melted butter over the inside. Pour in the beaten eggs and cook for 5 to 10 seconds, until they are just beginning to set very lightly on the bottom.

Immediately scrape the sides toward the middle, using the side of a fork. Carry on stirring almost constantly, gently shaking the pan with your other hand, until the omelet is cooked to your taste.

Allow 1 minute for a lightly cooked "runny" omelet; $1\frac{1}{2}$ minutes for a firm omelet, or 2 minutes if you prefer a well cooked omelet.

To roll the omelet, flip one half over toward the middle, while tilting the pan. Add the filling, if you are using one (see suggestions overleaf), then roll the omelet over itself completely. Roll the omelet onto a plate or serving platter. Using a knife tip, make an incision down the whole length to expose a little of the filling, then brush with a little melted butter.

suggested omelet fillings

I adore filled omelets; here are some of my favorite fillings, all to serve 2.

Mushroom omelet Slice 4oz (100g) white mushrooms and sauté in butter for 2 to 3 minutes with a little snipped Italian parsley or chives. When wild mushrooms are in season, use girolles or cèpes instead of white mushrooms.

Cheese omelet The classic cheese omelet is filled with grated Gruyère. However, I prefer to use fresh goat cheese. Lightly soften $2^1/_4$oz (60g) fresh goat cheese in a bain-marie, then mix with some halved and pitted black olives and spread over the half-rolled omelet before rolling it completely.

Lyonnaise omelet Cut 5oz (150g) peeled potatoes into small cubes and sauté in butter for 5 minutes. Add 5oz (150g) very thinly sliced onions and cook for another 6 to 8 minutes. Season with salt and pepper to taste and fill the omelet before rolling it.

Tomato and basil omelet Skin and seed 9oz (250g) tomatoes, chop into small pieces, and cook gently in 3 tbsp olive oil for 20 minutes. Season the cooked tomatoes with salt and pepper, add 5 or 6 snipped basil leaves, and spread the mixture over the omelet before rolling it.

Smoked salmon omelet with asparagus tips Cook 10oz (300g) asparagus spears in boiling salted water until the tips are cooked but still crisp. Drain and refresh in cold water, then cut off the stalks, keeping only the tips. Cut 4oz (100g) smoked salmon into wide strips and mix into the beaten eggs just before you cook the omelet. Warm the asparagus tips in 4 tbsp (50g) melted butter and fill the omelet before rolling it.

mussel & chive omelet

serves 2

$^1/_4$ cup (50ml) dry white wine
1 thyme sprig
16 fresh mussels, scrubbed
3 tbsp heavy cream
1 tbsp snipped chives
4 eggs
salt and freshly ground pepper
melted butter to brush (optional)

Put the wine, thyme, and mussels in a small pan, cover tightly, and cook for a few minutes until the mussels have steamed opened. Shell them immediately and place in a bowl, discarding any mussels that have not opened. Strain the juices through a cheesecloth-lined strainer into a small clean pan, to eliminate any sand.

Simmer the mussel juices over low heat until reduced by half, then add the cream and let it bubble until thick enough to coat the back of a spoon. Turn off the heat, add the chives and mussels, and keep warm (but not hot).

Beat the eggs in a bowl, season lightly, and use to make an omelet (see page 128). Half-roll it, then add the creamy mussels and push them into the middle with a spoon. Roll the omelet and slide it onto a warm large plate. To make it look even more appetizing, you could brush it with a little melted butter.

pear & cinnamon omelet

serves 2

1 very ripe large pear, or 2 small pears, about $8^{1}/_{2}$oz (240g) total weight
juice of $^{1}/_{2}$ lemon
4 tbsp (50g) butter
scant $^{1}/_{3}$ cup (60g) superfine sugar
1 tsp ground cinnamon
$^{1}/_{4}$ cup (50ml) white wine vinegar
4 eggs
salt and freshly ground pepper

Peel, halve, and core the pear(s), then cut into about 12 segments and toss with the lemon juice.

Melt the butter in a skillet, add the sugar, and cook over medium heat for about 2 minutes, until the butter and sugar amalgamate and boil to a pale caramel.

Add the pear segments, sprinkle with cinnamon, and cook in the buttery caramel, turning them delicately with a fork every few minutes. When they turn an amber caramel, add the wine vinegar and cook for another 3 minutes, until the caramel lightly coats the pears (see above). Set aside 4 good segments for the garnish.

Beat the eggs in a bowl, season lightly, and use to make an omelet (see page 128). Half-roll it and arrange the pear segments along its length. Roll up the omelet and slide it onto a plate. Arrange the 4 reserved pear segments on top and serve at once.

"This unusual omelet with 'pickled' pear will surprise and delight your taste buds. Serve it as an unexpected and harmonious appetizer."

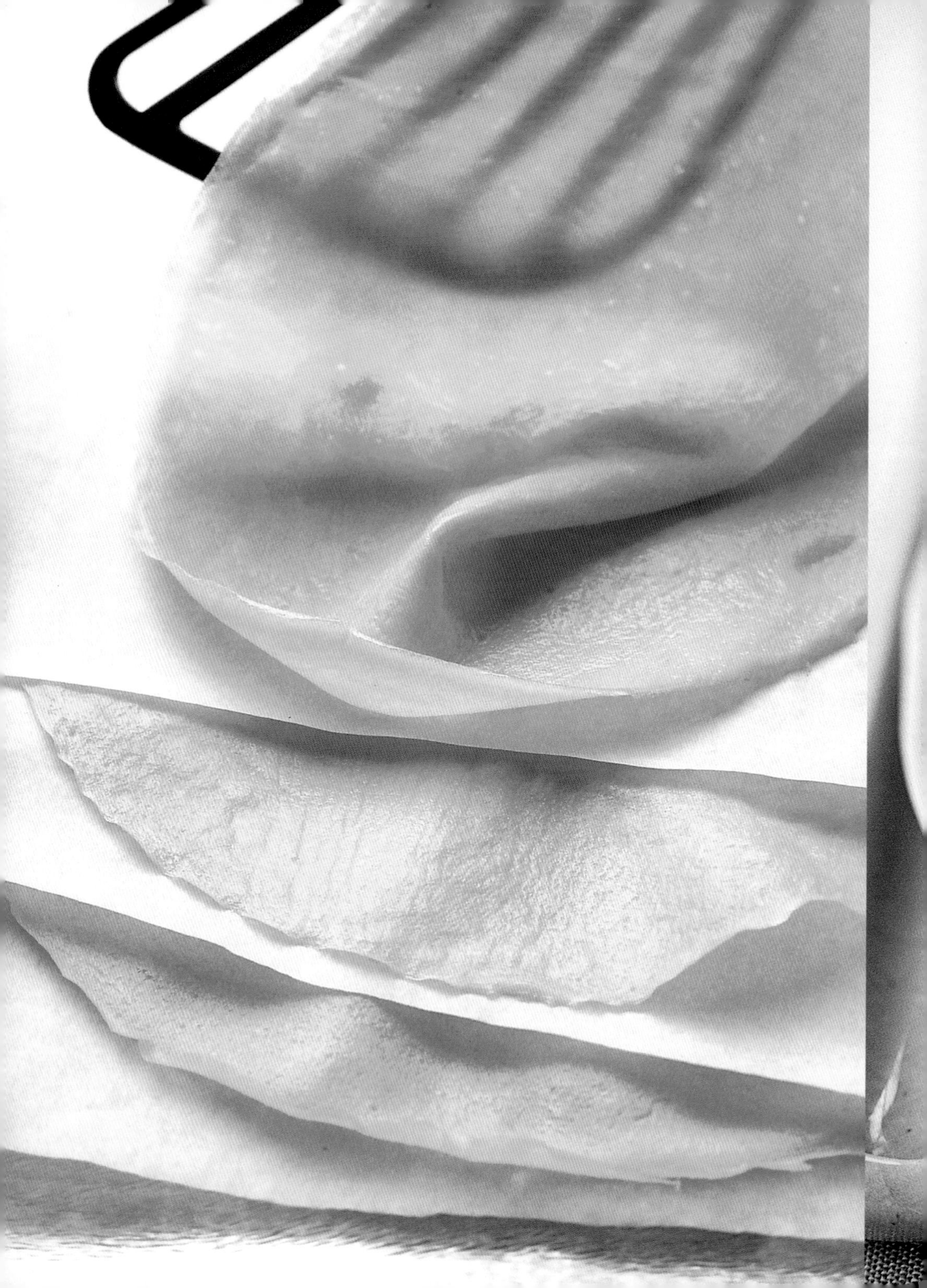

rolled thai omelets with shrimp on toast croûtes

serves 2

"These light, spicy canapés make a perfect prelude to dinner. Plain Thai omelets are also good rolled up, cut into thin strips, and mixed into a rice dish before serving, or added to a chicken broth."

1 large egg
1 tsp Thai fish sauce
2 scallions
2 tbsp (30g) softened butter
4 slices of white bread, 1/2 inch (1cm) thick
about 3 1/4oz (80g) shrimp, shelled
pinch of chile powder

Break the egg into a bowl, add the fish sauce, and beat very lightly. Very finely slice the green part of the scallions; set aside. Shred the top of the white scallions, keeping the base intact, then immerse in ice water to open out; set aside for the garnish. Drain and pat dry once they have opened.

Gently heat an 8-inch (20-cm) nonstick skillet with a very flat bottom, then brush with softened butter. Pour in half of the beaten egg and tilt to spread the egg thinly and evenly over the surface, as if making a crêpe. Cook over low heat for about 1 minute, until the omelet has set. Remove from the pan and slide onto a sheet of waxed paper or a plate. It should be cooked on one side only to keep it soft and malleable. Make another omelet with the rest of the egg in the same way.

To make the croûtes, cut out 4 circles from each slice of bread, using a 1 1/2-inch (4-cm) plain pastry cutter. Toast under the broiler on one side only.

Scatter the shelled shrimp and green scallion over the omelets and sprinkle with the chile powder. Roll each omelet up delicately but tightly to make an even roll. Cut each one into 8 small slices and stand them upright on the toasted side of the croûtes. Arrange on a serving dish and garnish with the white scallions.

illustrated on previous page

thai-style rolled omelet with smoked trout

serves 2

7oz (200g) new potatoes
small bunch of watercress, stalks removed
1 filleted smoked trout, 7oz (200g), skinned
2 large eggs
salt and freshly ground pepper
3tbsp (40g) softened butter
5tbsp olive oil
juice of 3 lemons
2 scallions, finely sliced
2tbsp heavy cream
1tbsp grated fresh horseradish

Boil the new potatoes in their skins for about 20 minutes until tender, then drain. Finely shred the watercress leaves, flake the smoked trout, and mix them together.

Break the eggs into a bowl, beat them very lightly, and season with salt. Gently heat an 8-inch (20-cm) nonstick skillet with a very flat bottom, then brush with a little softened butter. Pour one-quarter of the beaten egg into the pan and tilt to spread the egg thinly and evenly over the surface, as if you were making a crêpe. Cook over low heat for about 1 minute, until the omelet has set. Remove from the pan and slide onto a sheet of waxed paper or a plate. It should be cooked on one side only to keep it soft and malleable. Make three more omelets in the same way.

Peel the cooked potatoes and grate coarsely. Add the olive oil and the juice of 2 lemons, and season with salt and pepper. Add the scallions and mix delicately.

Spread the trout and watercress mixture delicately over the omelets. Mix the cream, remaining lemon juice, and the horseradish together, season to taste, and drizzle over the trout. Roll up the omelets gently but firmly and evenly. Divide the potato between 2 plates and arrange 2 omelets on each plate. Cut the omelets in half on the diagonal to reveal the filling. Serve as an appetizer or light lunch.

spanish tortilla with chorizo

serves 4

"A flat tortilla is almost identical to its Italian cousin, the frittata, but is generally thicker and therefore more rustic."

generous $^1/_3$ cup (100 ml) olive oil
14oz (400g) Russet potatoes, peeled and cubed
2 red onions, roughly chopped
salt and freshly ground pepper
7oz (200g) chorizo sausage, skinned
1 garlic clove, crushed
2 tbsp chopped Italian parsley leaves
6 eggs

Heat two-thirds of the olive oil in a skillet, 8–8½ inches (20–22cm) in diameter and 1½ inches (4cm) deep. When it is hot, put in the potatoes and cook over medium heat for 10 minutes. Add the onions, salt lightly, and cook for another 10 minutes or so.

In the meantime, cut the chorizo into $^1/_{16}$-inch (2-mm) slices. Add to the skillet with the garlic and parsley. Mix well, without crushing the potatoes, and cook for another 2 minutes. Tip everything onto a plate and let cool slightly. Wipe out the skillet with paper towels, ready for cooking the tortilla.

Lightly beat the eggs in a large bowl and season with salt and pepper. Heat the remaining olive oil in the skillet. Using a spoon, mix the eggs delicately into the cooled potato mixture, then pour into the pan. Start cooking over medium heat, stirring gently every few minutes with the side of a fork, as if making an omelet.

As soon as the eggs are half-cooked, stop stirring, and cook over very low heat for 2 to 3 minutes, until the underside of the tortilla is almost cooked. Slide it onto a lightly oiled platter, then invert it back into the pan and cook for another 2 minutes, until both sides are cooked the same and the middle of the tortilla is still soft.

Slide the tortilla onto a plate and serve it whole or cut into wedges. It is equally good served hot, warm, or at room temperature, but not chilled.

frittata of zucchini & confit tomato

serves 4

"This versatile frittata makes a delicious appetizer, but I sometimes serve it as a main course and simply double up all the ingredients. Cut it into small diamonds to make canapés or tapas packed with Mediterranean flavors."

confit tomatoes These complement many of my egg dishes. To prepare, skin 7oz (200g) very ripe tomatoes, preferably Roma, then halve or quarter and seed. Heat a generous 1 cup (250ml) light olive oil in a pan to 158°F (70°C), then add the tomatoes, 1 halved garlic clove, a pinch of crushed white peppercorns, a thyme sprig, and bay leaf. Cook at 158°F (70°C) for 10 to 15 minutes until tender, but not soft. The riper the tomatoes are, the less time they will take.

Leave the tomatoes to cool in the pan, then transfer to a jar or bowl. Cover with plastic wrap and keep in the refrigerator to use as required. Confit tomatoes will keep in the oil for at least 2 weeks. Just season them with salt and pepper before using. If you want to serve the tomatoes warm, place them under a low broiler briefly, or reheat in a pan with a splash of their oil for a few minutes.

illustrated on previous page

about 4½oz (120g) zucchini or patty pan squashes, trimmed
⅓ cup (100ml) olive oil, plus 2 tbsp to serve
6 eggs
salt and coarsely crushed pepper
7oz (200g) confit tomatoes (see left)
1 small thyme sprig, chopped
8 black olives, pitted (optional)
1 tbsp finely shredded Italian parsley leaves

Cut the zucchini into ½-inch (1-cm) slices or halve the patty pans. Heat two-thirds of the oil in a skillet, 8–8½ inches (20–22cm) in diameter and 1½ inches (4cm) deep. When hot, add the zucchini and cook over medium heat for 3 to 4 minutes.

In the meantime, lightly beat the eggs in a bowl and season sparingly with salt and pepper. Add the remaining oil, the confit tomatoes, thyme, and olives if using, to the pan. When everything is very hot, pour in the eggs and cook over medium heat, stirring gently every few minutes with the side of a fork, as if making an omelet.

As soon as the eggs are half-cooked, stop stirring, and cook over very low heat for 2 to 3 minutes, until the underside of the frittata is almost cooked. Slide it onto a lightly oiled plate, then invert it back into the pan and cook for another 2 minutes, still over low heat, until both sides are cooked the same and the frittata is still soft in the middle. Scatter the parsley over the surface.

Slide the frittata onto a serving plate and cut into wedges. Brush with a little olive oil, and serve some freshly crushed pepper on the side. It is equally good served hot, warm, or at room temperature.

frittata with artichokes & peppers

serves 4

6 small, very tender globe artichokes (the kind you can eat whole)
generous $^3/_4$ cup (180ml) olive oil
juice of 1 lemon
2 red bell peppers
1 red onion, chopped
leaves from 1 small thyme sprig
6 eggs
salt and freshly ground pepper

Trim $^3/_4$ inch (2cm) off the tips of the artichoke leaves, and all but $1^1/_4$ inch (3cm) off the stalks. Peel the attached stalk and remove 2 or 3 outer leaves unless tender. Mix half the oil and the lemon juice in a bowl. Quarter the artichokes and toss in the oil.

Skin the bell peppers with a vegetable peeler. Quarter, seed, and remove the pith, then lightly oil the flesh. Heat a griddle. Drain the artichokes and cook on the griddle with the peppers for 1 minute. Give them a quarter-turn and cook for another minute to mark a lattice. Turn them over and repeat on the other side. Transfer the peppers to a plate; cook the artichokes for another 2 to 3 minutes, then remove to the plate.

Heat 2tbsp oil in a skillet, 8–$8^1/_2$ inches (20–22cm) in diameter and $1^1/_2$ inches (4cm) deep. Add the onion and cook for 2 minutes to soften. Add the peppers, artichokes, and thyme, moisten with the remaining oil, and stir for 3 to 4 minutes.

Lightly beat the eggs with a little salt, pour them into the pan, and cook over medium heat, stirring gently every few minutes with the side of a fork, as if making an omelet. As soon as the eggs are half-cooked, stop stirring, and finish the cooking over very low heat for 2 to 3 minutes, until the underside of the frittata is almost cooked.

Slide onto a lightly oiled plate, invert back into the pan, and cook gently for another 2 minutes; the frittata should still be soft in the middle. Slide onto a plate.

“Cut the frittata into wedges, or into small squares to serve as tapas. It is equally good hot, warm, or at room temperature, but not chilled.”

soufflés

Making a soufflé should be a pleasure and ultimately rewarding, but if the idea fills you with dread, here are a few hints for success. The egg whites should be neither too fresh or too cold, or they will not rise very well. I use the whites of medium eggs; if you are unsure of the size, check the volume (see page 12). Don't use a plastic bowl for whisking as plastic retains grease, the enemy of egg whites. Once the whites are half-whisked, add a pinch of salt for savory soufflés or a little sugar for sweet ones; this will help to maintain their volume. When you fold in the whites, make sure the mixture is hot or warm, never cold or you won't be able to incorporate the whites evenly without overworking. Finally, when the soufflé is in the oven, don't keep opening the door every few minutes—soufflés detest drafts and are likely to collapse!

classic gruyère soufflés

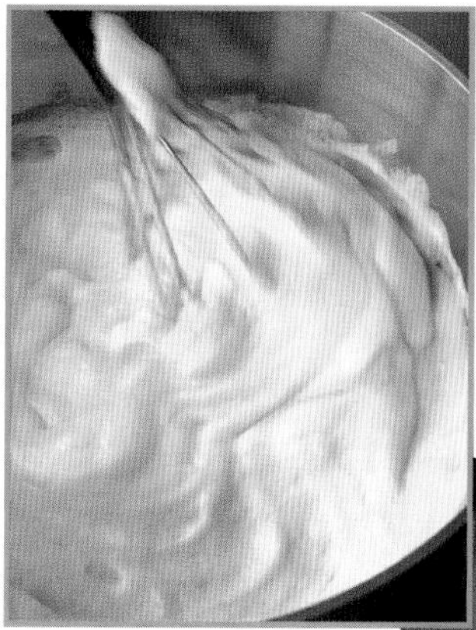

This technique is similar for all hot soufflés—savory and sweet.

Preheat the oven to 400°F (200°C). Beat the egg whites with a pinch of salt until soft peaks form.

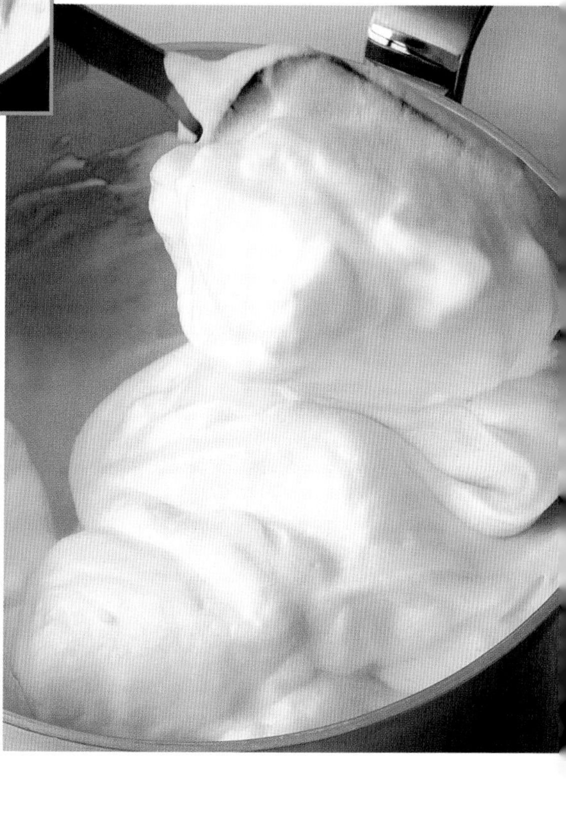

4 tbsp (50g) softened butter, to grease dishes
2 oz (50g) Gruyère, grated, to coat dishes
$1\frac{1}{2}$ tbsp (20g) butter
2 tbsp (20g) all-purpose flour
generous 1 cup (250ml) milk
salt and freshly ground pepper
pinch of cayenne
6 medium egg yolks
10 medium egg whites
$8\frac{1}{2}$ oz (240g) Gruyère, finely grated, plus 8 or 4 thin disks

Generously grease the insides of 8 standard $3\frac{1}{4}$ inch (8 cm) ramekins (or four 4-inch (10-cm) soufflé dishes) with the softened butter. Put about $\frac{1}{2}$ cup (50 g) grated Gruyère into one dish, rotate it to coat the inside, then tip the excess into another ramekin. Repeat to coat them all.

To make the béchamel, melt the $1\frac{1}{2}$ tbsp butter in a pan. Add the flour and cook for 2 minutes, stirring with a whisk, to make a roux. Still stirring, add the cold milk and bring to a boil over medium heat. Let bubble for a minute or two, then pour the béchamel into a bowl. Season lightly with salt, pepper, and cayenne, then whisk in the egg yolks. Cover with plastic wrap and let cool slightly.

Immediately mix one-third of the egg whites into the warm soufflé mixture with a whisk, then, using a large spoon, fold in the rest with one hand while showering in the grated Gruyère with the other. Stop as soon as the mixture is amalgamated.

Spoon the mixture into the ramekins to come 1/4 inch (5 mm) above the rim. Smooth the surface, then use a knife tip to ease the mixture away from the side of each ramekins to help it rise.

Stand the ramekins in a deep ovenproof dish lined with a sheet of waxed paper and pour in enough almost-boiling water to come halfway up the sides. Bake the soufflés for 4 minutes (or 6 minutes for 4-inch (10-cm) dishes). Meanwhile, trim the Gruyère disks to the same diameter as the dishes and cut into 4 segments. Quickly position a segmented Gruyère disk on top of each soufflé and immediately return to the oven for 1 minute (or 2 minutes for 4-inch (10-cm) dishes). Put the cooked soufflés on individual plates and serve at once—they won't wait!

NOTES These classic soufflés are perfect appetizers. If I'm serving a three-course meal, I make them in individual 4-inch (10-cm) soufflé dishes. If they are going to followed by a number of courses, I use ramekins, which offer just 4 or 5 delicious mouthfuls. Comté cheese has a fuller, stronger flavor than Gruyère and can be used instead. The choice is yours.

For all sweet soufflés (chocolate, vanilla, mango, etc), whisk the egg whites with a pinch of sugar rather than a pinch of salt.

I always allow generous quantities of mixture for my individual soufflés, so don't worry if you have some left over after filling the ramekins—better safe than sorry!

Roquefort & walnut soufflés Follow the recipe for classic Gruyère soufflés, coating the dishes with fine white bread crumbs rather than grated cheese. Replace the 8½oz (240g) Gruyère or Comté with about 5½oz (160g) chilled Roquefort, cut into small pieces. (This should not be too soft or overripe.) Fold into the béchamel with the egg whites, then fold in 12 coarsely chopped walnuts, and finally 4 finely diced fresh, very ripe figs. Bake as directed (see left) and serve immediately, with a salad of corn salad and thick sticks of apple (preferably Granny Smith), dressed with a well-seasoned vinaigrette.

cheddar, sorrel & anchovy soufflés

makes 4

"The creamy texture of this soufflé conceals a surprise element—the shredded sorrel. Its slight acidity is a perfect foil for the anchovies. When sorrel is not in season, use spinach instead."

4 tbsp (50g) softened butter, to grease dishes
2 oz (50g) Cheddar, grated, to coat dishes
1½ tbsp (20g) butter
2 tbsp (20g) all-purpose flour
generous 1 cup (250ml) milk
salt and freshly ground pepper
6 medium egg yolks
1 tbsp anchovy essence
10 medium egg whites
½ oz (15g) sorrel leaves, shredded
7 oz (200g) Cheddar, grated, plus extra 1½ tbsp
4 anchovy fillets in oil, drained

Butter four 4-inch (10-cm) soufflé dishes and coat the insides with grated cheese.

To make the béchamel, melt the butter in a small pan, add the flour, and cook, stirring, for 2 minutes. Still stirring, add the milk and bring to a boil over medium heat. Let bubble for a minute or two, then pour into a bowl. Season very lightly with salt and plenty of pepper, and whisk in the egg yolks, then the anchovy essence. Cover the bowl with plastic wrap; let cool slightly.

Preheat the oven to 400°F (200°C). Beat the egg whites with a pinch of salt until soft peaks form. Immediately mix one-third of the egg whites into the warm soufflé mixture with a whisk, then, using a large spoon, fold in the rest with one hand while showering in the sorrel and 2 cups (200g) grated Cheddar with the other. Stop as soon as the mixture is completely amalgamated.

Spoon the mixture into the soufflé dishes to come ¼ inch (5 mm) above the rim. Bake the soufflés for 6 minutes, then sprinkle the tops with a little grated Cheddar and immediately return to the oven for another 2 minutes. Top each soufflé with a rolled anchovy fillet and serve immediately.

langoustine soufflés with shellfish coulis

makes 8

8 fine langoustines
salt and freshly ground pepper
2 tbsp peanut oil
4 white mushrooms, sliced
3 shallots, very thinly sliced
2 tarragon sprigs
2½ cups (600ml) ready-made fish stock (bought fresh stock is fine)
4 tbsp (50g) softened butter, to grease
1½ tbsp (20g) butter
2 tbsp (20g) all-purpose flour
pinch of cayenne
4 medium egg yolks
5 tbsp (75ml) heavy cream
1 tbsp cognac or Armagnac (optional)
8 medium egg whites

Add the langoustines to a pan of boiling salted water and cook for 4 minutes. Drain and shell the langoustines when they are cool enough to handle. Cut the tail meat into ½-inch (1-cm) pieces, place in a bowl, and cover with plastic wrap. Split the heads lengthwise with a heavy knife and use for the stock.

Heat the oil in a pan, add the langoustine heads, and cook over medium heat to color them, stirring every minute. Add the mushrooms, shallots, and tarragon, and sweat gently for 5 minutes. Add the fish stock and cook over medium heat until reduced almost by half. Pass the stock through a chinois or fine strainer, pushing with the back of a ladle to extract as much flavor as you can from the langoustine heads. Put the stock to one side to cool slightly.

Butter the insides of 8 deep 3¼-inch (8-cm) ramekins, about 2½ inches (6cm) high. Melt the butter in a small pan, add the flour. and cook for 2 minutes, stirring constantly with a whisk, to make a roux. Still stirring, add a scant 1 cup (220ml) of the langoustine stock and bring to a boil over medium heat. Let it bubble gently for a minute or two, then pour into a bowl. Season lightly with salt and a pinch of cayenne, and whisk in the egg yolks. Cover the bowl with plastic wrap and let cool slightly.

illustrated on previous page

"A springtime specialty at The Waterside Inn, these soufflés are immensely popular and certainly merit the time taken to prepare them … once tasted, never forgotten."

To make the shellfish coulis, put the rest of the langoustine stock into a small pan and bring to a boil. Immediately add the cream, and the cognac if using, and let bubble for 2 minutes, then season with salt and pepper to taste; keep hot.

Preheat the oven to 400°F (200°C). Beat the egg whites with a pinch of salt until soft peaks form. Immediately mix one-third into the warm soufflé mixture with a whisk, then, using a large spoon, fold in the rest until evenly incorporated. Half-fill the ramekins with the mixture. Gently warm the langoustine tails and divide them between the dishes, then fill up with soufflé mixture to come 1/4 inch (5 mm) above the rim.

Stand the ramekins in a deep ovenproof dish lined with a sheet of waxed paper and pour in enough almost-boiling water to come halfway up the sides. Bake for 6 minutes until well risen and golden.

Take these very light and delicate soufflés to the table straight from the oven. Make a little slit in the middle with a knife tip and pour in the hot langoustine coulis to serve.

bacon & parsley soufflés with eggs "en surprise"

makes 4

"These little soufflés are ideal for lunch or brunch. The mingling of the yolk from the surprise poached egg with the soufflé is a treat. A tomato coulis on the side goes well, but it is not essential."

4 tbsp (50g) softened butter, to grease dishes
2oz (50g) Gruyère or Comté, grated, to coat
1½ tbsp (20g) butter
2 tbsp (20g) all-purpose flour
generous 1 cup (250ml) milk
salt and freshly ground pepper
6 medium egg yolks
about 5½oz (160g) bacon, thinly sliced, cut into ¼-inch (5-mm) wide small strips
1 tbsp peanut oil
8 medium egg whites
¾oz (20g) Italian parsley, finely snipped
4 poached eggs (see page 44)

Butter four 4-inch (10-cm) soufflé dishes and coat the insides with grated cheese.

To make the béchamel, melt the butter in a small pan, add the flour, and cook, stirring, for 2 minutes. Still stirring, add the milk and bring to a boil over medium heat. Let bubble for a minute or two, then pour into a bowl. Season lightly, then whisk in the egg yolks. Cover the bowl with plastic wrap; let cool slightly.

Put the bacon in a pan, cover with water, bring to a boil, and boil for 30 seconds. Remove, refresh, drain well, and pat dry. Heat the oil in a nonstick skillet and brown the bacon strips over high heat for 1 minute, then drain and set aside.

Preheat the oven to 400°F (200°C). Beat the egg whites with a pinch of salt until soft peaks form. Immediately mix one-third into the warm soufflé mixture with a whisk, then, using a large spoon, fold in the rest with one hand while showering in the bacon and parsley with the other. Stop as soon as the mixture is amalgamated.

Heat the poached eggs in boiling water for 30 seconds, then drain well. Two-thirds fill the soufflé dishes with the soufflé mixture. Carefully place a poached egg in the center of each dish, then fill up with mixture to come ¼ inch (5mm) above the rim. Stand the dishes in a bain-marie. Cook for 8 minutes, then serve immediately.

chocolate soufflés

makes 4

"These are heavenly! To make them even more divine, slip a spoonful of freshly churned vanilla ice cream (see page 238) into the center of each soufflé at the table."

3 tbsp (40g) softened butter, to grease dishes
1/4 cup (40g) superfine sugar, to coat dishes
1/2 cup (50g) unsweetened cocoa, sifted
8 1/2 oz (240g) semisweet chocolate (70% cocoa solids), chopped into small pieces
10 medium egg whites
1/4 cup (40g) superfine sugar

for the pastry cream

1 3/4 cups (350ml) milk
generous 1/3 cup (80g) superfine sugar
4 medium egg yolks
scant 1/4 cup (30g) all-purpose flour

to finish

confectioners' sugar, to dust

Butter four 4-inch (10-cm) soufflé dishes and coat the insides with the sugar.

To make the pastry cream, put the milk and two-thirds of the sugar in a small pan and slowly bring to a boil. Put the egg yolks and remaining sugar in a bowl and whisk to a ribbon consistency, then incorporate the flour. Pour the hot milk onto the yolks, stirring constantly with a whisk. Return to the pan and whisk over low heat for 1 minute. Pour into a bowl, cover with plastic wrap, and let cool slightly.

Preheat the oven to 400°F (200°C) and put a baking sheet inside to heat. Measure 10oz (280g) of the pastry cream and delicately mix in the cocoa and chopped chocolate using a whisk. (Keep the rest of the pastry cream for another use.)

Beat the egg whites to a thick foam, then add the 1/4 cup (40g) sugar and continue to beat until soft peaks form. Fold one-third into the pastry cream using a whisk, then delicately fold in the rest with a large spoon; the mixture will be fairly loose.

Divide the mixture between the soufflé dishes, filling them to the top. Stand on the hot baking sheet and cook for 10 minutes. As you take the soufflés out of the oven, dust the tops with confectioners' sugar, place on warm plates, and serve at once.

vanilla & mango soufflés with passion fruit coulis

makes 4

3 tbsp (40g) softened butter, to grease dishes
1/4 cup (40g) superfine sugar, to coat dishes
8 medium egg whites
generous 1/3 cup (80g) superfine sugar
1 very ripe mango, about 14 oz (400g), peeled, pitted, and finely diced

for the pastry cream
1 3/4 cups (350ml) milk
scant 1/3 cup (70g) superfine sugar
1 vanilla bean, split lengthwise
7 medium egg yolks
generous 1/3 cup (50g) all-purpose flour

for the passion fruit coulis
2 tbsp (30g) superfine sugar
juice of 2 oranges
2 passion fruit, halved

Butter 4 individual 4-inch (10-cm) soufflé dishes and coat the insides with the sugar. To make the coulis, boil the sugar and orange juice until reduced by one-third, pour into a bowl, and let cool. Scrape the passion fruit seeds into the cold syrup; set aside.

For the pastry cream, put the milk and 1/4 cup (40g) sugar in a small pan, scrape in the seeds from the vanilla bean, and slowly bring to a boil. Whisk the egg yolks and remaining sugar in a bowl to a ribbon consistency, then incorporate the flour. Pour the hot milk onto the yolks, stirring with a whisk. Return to the pan and whisk over low heat for 1 minute, then pour into a bowl, cover with plastic wrap, and cool slightly.

Preheat the oven to 400°F (200°C) and put a baking sheet inside to heat. Beat the egg whites to a thick foam, then add the 1/3 cup (80g) sugar and continue to beat until they form soft peaks. Fold one-third into the pastry cream using a whisk, then delicately fold in the rest with a large spoon, scattering in the diced mango as you go.

Divide the mixture between the soufflé dishes, to come level with the rim. Stand on the hot baking sheet and cook for 8 minutes. Serve the soufflés as soon as they come out of the oven on warm plates, with the coulis in a sauce boat. Invite guests to make a small well in the middle of their soufflé with a little spoon and pour in a little coulis.

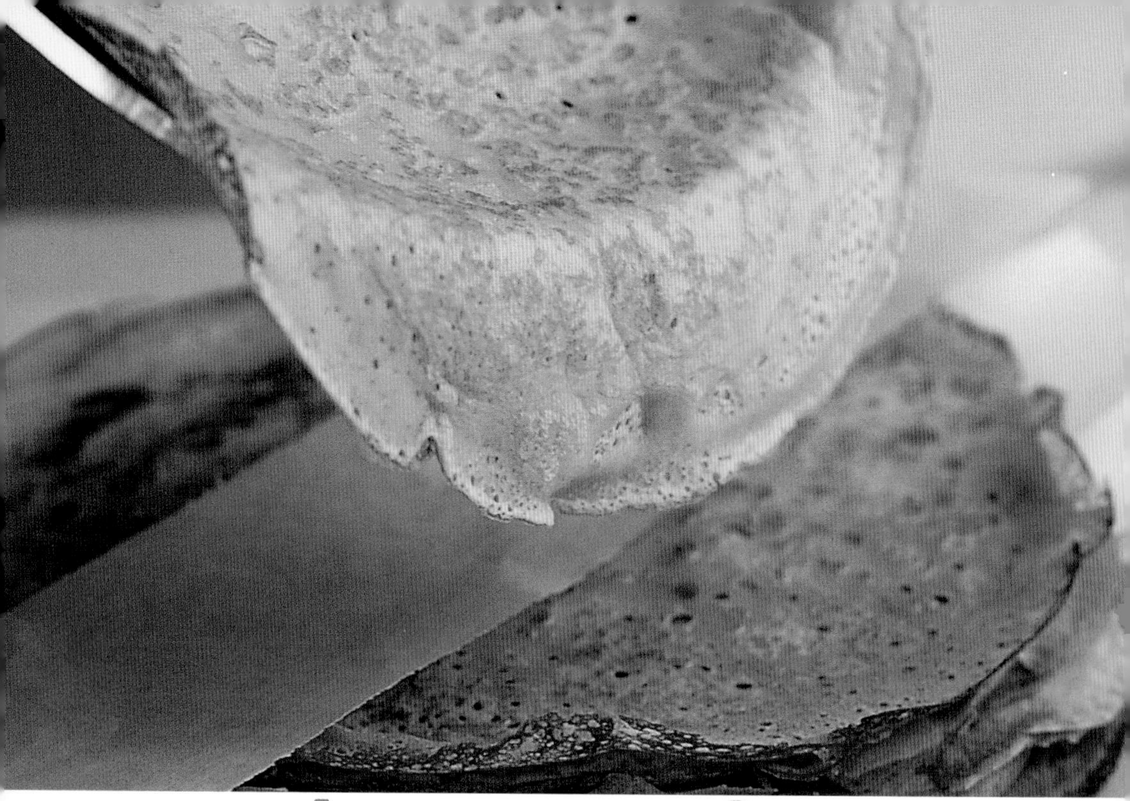

crêpes & batters

Fortunately, my mother was an excellent cook who loved making crêpes for us. Shortly after the war, when I was quite small, she would make a batter with the few eggs she had, lots of flour to fill us up, and milk diluted with water. The resulting crêpes were very thick to keep us sustained, but as things improved over the years, they became finer and finer, until almost like lace. Nowadays, I love making crêpes and waffles for my grandchildren. They all help to prepare the batter and join in with the cooking. Today, crêperies are everywhere, offering pancakes made from different flours like buckwheat or rye, and enclosing a myriad of savory and sweet fillings. Batters can be made a day ahead and kept in a container in the refrigerator until needed. From fritters to Yorkshire puddings and clafoutis, they offer a palette of different textures.

crêpes makes 16–18

scant 1 cup (125g) all-purpose flour
1 tbsp (15g) superfine sugar
pinch of salt
2 eggs
generous 1¼ cups (325ml) milk
generous ⅓ cup (100ml) heavy cream
few drops of vanilla extract or orange flower water, or a little grated lemon zest
a little oil, to cook

To make the batter, put the flour, sugar, and salt in a bowl. Add the eggs, mix well with a whisk, then stir in a generous ⅓ cup (100ml) milk to make a smooth batter. Gradually stir in the rest of the milk and the cream. Let the batter rest in a warm place for about an hour.

When you are ready to cook the crêpes, give the batter a stir and flavor with vanilla, orange flower water, or lemon zest. Brush an $8^1/_2$-inch (22-cm) crêpe pan with a little oil and heat. Ladle in a little batter and tilt the pan to cover the bottom thinly. Cook the crêpe for 1 minute.

As soon as little holes appear all over the surface, turn the crêpe over and cook the other side for 30 to 40 seconds. Transfer to a plate and cook the rest of the batter, stacking the crêpes interleaved with waxed paper as they are cooked.

Roll up the crêpes, or fold in half or into quarters and eat immediately, either just as they are, dusted with sugar, or filled.

crêpes with summer berries

serves 6

1 quantity crêpe batter (see page 168)
generous 1 cup (150g) raspberries
generous 1 cup (150g) blackberries
6 small mint sprigs
confectioners' sugar, to dust
for the red berry coulis
1/4 cup (50g) sugar
1 2/3 cups (200g) raspberries or strawberries
juice of 1/2 lemon

First make the red berry coulis. Put the sugar and 1/4 cup (50ml) water in a pan and set over low heat until the sugar has dissolved. Increase the heat and boil the sugar syrup for 3 minutes, then remove and let cool. When cold, put the sugar syrup in a blender with the berries and lemon juice, and whiz for 1 minute, then pass the coulis through a chinois or fine strainer into a bowl.

Cook the crêpes (see page 169). Put a warm crêpe on each plate and sprinkle on some raspberries and blackberries. Cover with another crêpe and partially fold it back over itself. Spoon on little dabs of red berry coulis, add a sprig of mint, dust with confectioners' sugar, and serve at once.

Put the remaining crêpes, berries, and red berry coulis on the table for people to help themselves.

illustrated on previous page

crêpes with apples & candied kumquats

serves 4

4 warm crêpes (see page 168)
2 slightly tart apples (such as McIntosh or Rome Beauty)
2 tbsp (30g) butter
8 candied kumquats (see page 275)
confectioners' sugar, to dust

Prepare the filling before you cook the crêpes. Peel and core the apples, cut into segments, and put in a pan with the butter and $^1/_4$ cup (50 ml) water. Stew until soft, then purée using a hand-held blender to make a smooth compote.

Cut the kumquats into $^1/_{16}$-inch (2–3-mm) thick circles and mix them into the warm apple compote. Spread over the middle of the crêpes, then roll them up.

Put a filled crêpe on each warm plate and dust lightly with confectioners' sugar. Serve at once.

"I like to serve these tempting crêpes with a vanilla crème anglaise (see page 216) for an indulgent treat."

savory crêpes with seasonal crudités

serves 4

½ quantity crêpe batter (see page 168), without sugar or flavorings
1–2 tsp snipped Italian parsley leaves

for the filling

5 oz (150 g) carrots, grated
2 oz (50 g) red onion or shallots, chopped
generous ¼ cup (50 g) golden raisins
¼ cup (30 g) pine nuts, toasted
2 hard-cooked eggs (see page 19), chopped
2 tbsp snipped Italian parsley leaves
5 tbsp peanut oil
2 tbsp wine vinegar
salt and freshly ground pepper

to serve

lemon wedges

First prepare the filling. Mix the grated carrot with the chopped onion. Blanch the golden raisins in boiling water for 10 seconds, then refresh in cold water and drain well. Add to the carrot mixture with the toasted pine nuts and mix well.

Flavor the chopped hard-cooked eggs with the 2 tbsp snipped parsley.

Whisk the oil with the wine vinegar and seasoning to make a vinaigrette. Toss the carrot mixture in the vinaigrette. Check the seasoning.

Flavor the crêpe batter with a little snipped parsley, then cook 8 crêpes (see page 169). Arrange a crêpe on each of 4 plates. Spread the carrot mixture on top, cover each with another crêpe, and sprinkle the chopped egg on top. Serve cold, with lemon wedges.

"To vary the filling, replace the carrot with freshly grated celeriac or beet."

chicken & mushrooms crêpes

serves 4

$^1/_2$ quantity crêpe batter (see page 168), without sugar or flavorings
1–2 tsp snipped Italian parsley leaves

for the filling

2 boneless chicken breasts, 5–7 oz (150–200g) each
scant 1 cup (200ml) chicken stock
3 tbsp (40g) butter
5 oz (150g) small white mushrooms, sliced
juice of $^1/_2$ lemon
salt and freshly ground pepper
4 tbsp snipped Italian parsley leaves (optional)
1 quantity hot Mornay sauce (see page 299)

First make the filling. Remove the skin from the chicken breasts and place them in a pan. Pour on the chicken stock and bring to a simmer. Lower the heat and poach gently for 10 minutes (the stock should barely tremble). Leave the chicken to cool in the liquor.

Melt the butter in a skillet, add the mushrooms, and cook over medium heat for 2 to 3 minutes. Add the lemon juice, season with salt and pepper, and scatter over the parsley if using. Transfer to a bowl.

Cut the chicken breasts into thick strips and mix with the mushrooms. Tip the mixture into the hot Mornay sauce, stir, and adjust the seasoning.

Flavor the crêpe batter with a little snipped parsley, then cook 4 crêpes (see page 169), each about $10^1/_2$ inches (26cm) diameter and a touch thicker than usual.

Put a warm crêpe on each warmed plate. Divide the filling between the crêpes, spooning it more generously onto the part furthest from you. Fold over the sides to form a cornet shape. Serve with corn salad on the side.

waffles

serves 6

"Everyone loves waffles, but you will need a waffle iron to make your own."

for the waffle batter
scant $1^1/_4$ cups (160g) all-purpose flour
1 tbsp (15g) superfine sugar, plus extra pinch
pinch of salt
4 tbsp (50g) butter, melted
2 eggs, separated
generous 1 cup (270ml) milk
few drops of vanilla extract or orange flower water, or a little grated lemon zest

to cook and serve
$1^1/_2$ tbsp (20g) butter, softened
confectioners' or superfine sugar, to dust, or honey or maple syrup

To make the waffle batter, combine the flour, 1 tbsp (15g) sugar, salt, melted butter, egg yolks, and about one-third of the milk in a bowl. Whisk lightly until smooth, then gradually whisk in the rest of the milk. Add your chosen flavoring, cover the bowl with plastic wrap, and set aside while you heat the waffle iron (for 5 to 10 minutes before cooking).

In a small bowl, whisk the egg whites with a pinch of sugar to a thick foam (but not to peaks). Gently fold into the waffle batter, using a balloon whisk.

Lightly brush the waffle iron with softened butter, then ladle in enough batter to cover the griddle. Close the lid and cook for 3 to 4 minutes, until the waffles are cooked to your liking. Some like them dry and crisp; others soft and lightly colored. Cook the rest of the batter in the same way. Don't bother to grease the waffle iron each time; you only need to do this every third or fourth waffle.

Serve the waffles immediately on warm plates or a large platter. Dust with confectioners' or superfine sugar, or drizzle with a little honey or maple syrup.

"For a decadent finish, top with ice cream or a generous spoonful of Chiboust cream (see page 221) and blueberries."

cherry clafoutis

serves 8

8 tbsp (100g) butter
3/4lb (350g) ripe cherries, pitted
for the batter
2 eggs
generous 1/2 cup (80g) all-purpose flour
6 1/2 tbsp (80g) butter, melted and cooled
1/3 cup (60g) granulated sugar, plus extra
2/3 cup (150ml) cold milk
1 vanilla bean, split lengthwise
1 tbsp Kirsch (optional)

To make the batter, very lightly beat the eggs in a bowl with a fork and add the flour. Whisk in the melted butter, then gradually mix in the granulated sugar and milk. Use a knife tip to scrape the vanilla seeds into the batter, and add the Kirsch if using.

Preheat the oven to 400°F (200°C). Use about 5 tbsp (60g) of the butter to generously grease an 8-inch (20-cm) diameter, 2-inch (5-cm) deep ovenproof dish. Spread the cherries in the bottom, then pour the batter over them.

Carefully place in the hot oven, making sure that the batter doesn't spill over the top. Bake for 10 minutes, then lower the oven setting to 350°F (180°C). Cut the remaining butter into small pieces, dot them over the top of the clafoutis, and bake for another 25 minutes or so.

To check if the clafoutis is cooked, delicately slide in a knife tip. If it comes out smooth and clean, the clafoutis is ready. Dust with a little granulated sugar and let stand for a few minutes. Serve the clafoutis warm, from the dish.

"You can use other soft-fleshed seasonal fruits, such as greengages, mirabelles, blackberries, and pears. A spoonful of appropriate eau-de-vie or liqueur is the cherry on the cake."

illustrated on previous page

apple & pear fritters

serves 4

"Dip these sweet fritters into a red berry coulis (see page 172) and they are even more tempting. Other fruits, such as bananas and pineapple, also make excellent fritters."

1/8 oz (5g) fresh yeast
2 1/2 cups (600ml) milk
3/4 cup (100g) all-purpose flour
1/4 cup (50ml) light beer
1 egg yolk
pinch of salt
1 tbsp peanut oil
1 apple, preferably Granny Smith
1 pear, preferably Bartlett
juice of 1 lemon

to cook and serve

peanut oil, to deep-fry
1 1/2 medium egg whites
pinch of superfine sugar, plus extra to dust

To make the fritter batter, whisk the yeast with half of the milk in a small bowl. Combine the flour, beer, the remaining milk, egg yolk, and salt in a large bowl and whisk lightly until smooth. Pour in the yeast liquid and the 1 tbsp oil, mix well, then cover with plastic wrap and let stand for 2 hours.

Peel the apple and pear, cut each into 8 or 10 segments, removing the core, and sprinkle with lemon juice. Heat the oil for deep-frying in a suitable pan to 325°F (170°C). In a small bowl, whisk the egg whites with a pinch of sugar to a thick foam (but not to peaks), then delicately fold into the batter, using a spatula.

Cook the fritters in batches. One at a time, lift the apple segments with a fork, dip into the batter to coat, then drop them into the hot oil. Deep-fry for 3 to 4 minutes until lightly colored, turning them over with the tip of the fork tines to color both sides; the fritters will rise to the surface when they are cooked.

Remove and drain on paper towels. Cook the pear segments in the same way, allowing 2 to 3 minutes cooking only, as these are more tender than the apples. Serve the fritters as soon as they are all cooked, but take care—they will be very hot. Sprinkle with superfine sugar as you serve them.

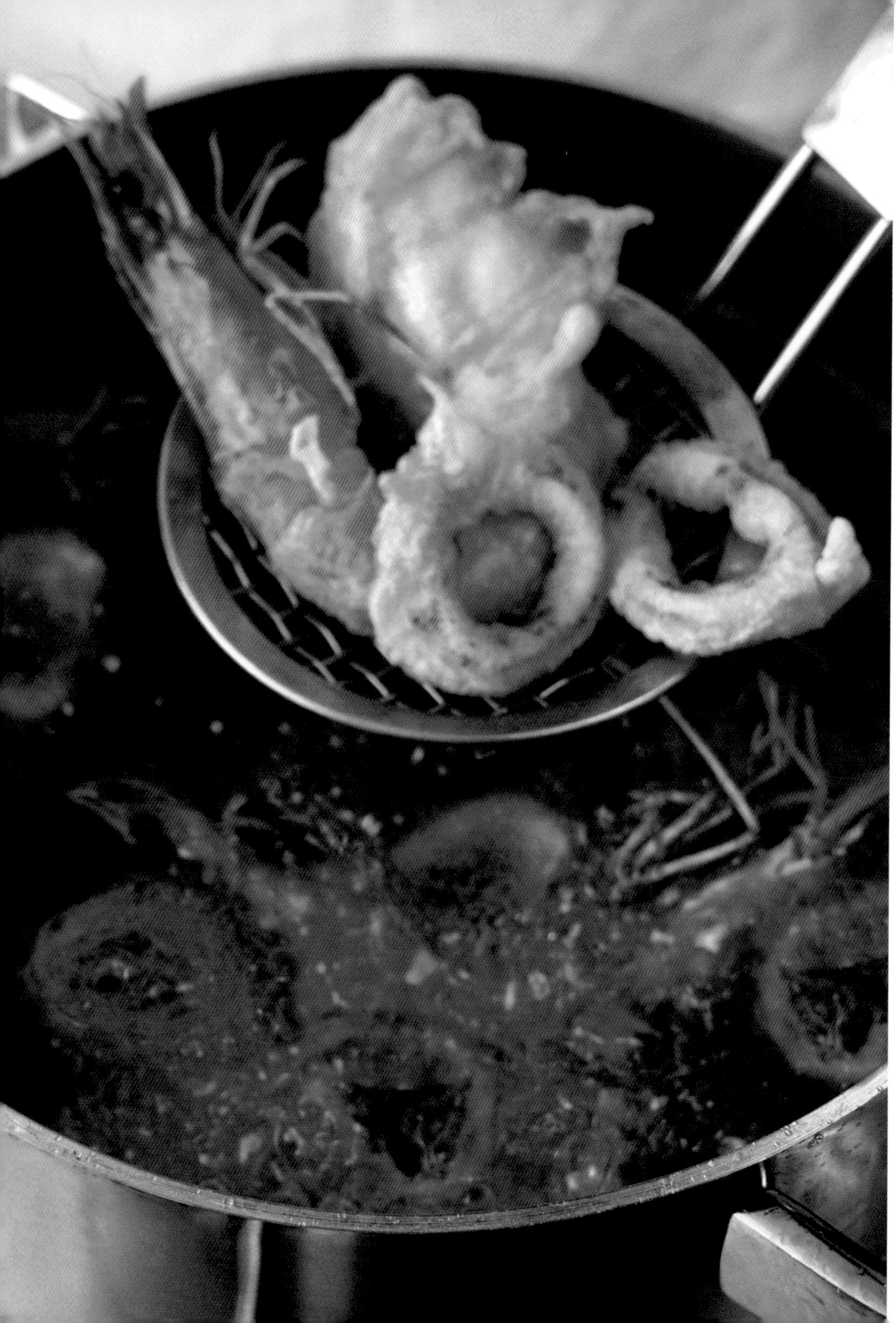

seafood & monkfish fritters

serves 4

"This light, crunchy fritter batter is perfect for seafood and fish, as it provides a delicate coating."

3/4 cup (100g) all-purpose flour
1/4 cup (50ml) white wine vinegar
1 medium egg
salt and freshly ground pepper
8 large raw shrimp
1 squid, about 7oz (200g), cleaned
4 monkfish medallions, about 3oz (75g) each

to cook and serve
peanut oil, to deep-fry
1 lemon, cut into quarters

To make the fritter batter, put the flour in a bowl, then add a generous 1/3 cup (100ml) cold water, the wine vinegar, and egg, and mix with a whisk. Season with a very little salt and pepper. Cover with plastic wrap and let stand for 20 minutes.

Shell the shrimp tails, leaving the heads attached. Cut the squid pouch into rings, rinse, and pat dry. Do not rinse the monkfish medallions, but pat them dry.

To cook the fritters, heat the oil in a suitable pan to 350°F (180°C). Deep-fry the fish in batches. One at a time, lift the squid rings with a fork, dunk them into the batter to coat, then drop into the hot oil and fry for 2 minutes. As soon as the fritters are cooked, lift them out with a slotted spoon and drain on paper towels.

Repeat with the monkfish medallions, allowing 3 to 4 minutes deep-frying. Hold the shell heads in your fingers near the antennae, and dip only the tails into the batter. Put them into the hot oil carefully so that it doesn't splutter and deep-fry for about 2 minutes.

Serve the fritters straightaway, with lemon wedges. You might also like to serve a mayonnaise on the side for dipping.

yorkshires with caramelized onions & sausages

serves 6

for the yorkshire batter
2 eggs
½ cup (70g) all-purpose flour
scant 1 cup (200ml) lowfat milk
salt and freshly ground pepper
for the filling
6½ tbsp (80g) butter
1 large onion, 10oz (300g), very thinly sliced
⅓ cup (100ml) beef drippings, or ⅓ cup (100ml) peanut oil
2 tbsp peanut oil
18 cocktail sausages, blanched
pinch of sugar

To make the batter, lightly whisk the eggs in a bowl, then whisk in the flour a little at a time, until smooth. Slowly add the milk, stirring with the whisk, and season with a little salt and pepper. Cover and refrigerate the batter for at least 2 hours.

Preheat the oven to 425°F (220°C). For the filling, melt the butter in a pan and gently cook the onion for 30 minutes, stirring every 5 minutes, until meltingly soft.

Put a little drippings or oil into each of 6 Yorkshire pudding molds or muffin pans and place in the oven for 4 to 5 minutes until the fat starts to smoke. Give the batter a stir, then ladle it into the molds until it almost reaches the top. Bake for 25 minutes or until golden brown and crisp, but still slightly soft in the middle.

In the meantime, heat the oil in a skillet and cook the sausages for 3 to 4 minutes, until golden; keep warm. Sprinkle the onion with the sugar, increase the heat slightly, and cook, stirring, until lightly caramelized.

Unmold the Yorkshire puddings onto a wire rack, taking care not to burn yourself, then place one on each warm plate. Fill the cavities with the caramelized onion and sausages. Serve piping hot.

egg-rich pastry & pasta

Egg-rich pastries form the basis of delicious quiches, tarts, and tartlets. To ensure that the pastry shells are baked to perfection, the tart pie dough must be rolled out as thinly as possible—an 1/8 inch (2–3mm) thickness is ideal. A thick, undercooked shell will ruin a tart, however delicious the filling. Choux paste is mainly associated with desserts but it also forms the basis of mouthwatering gougères (see page 192), which I serve as canapés at The Waterside Inn. Pasta is simple to make and cut, using a pasta machine, and tastes far better than commercial varieties. If you do not own a pasta machine, I strongly recommend you buy one. Everyone loves pasta, and you can create an endless variety of tempting meals, by flavoring it with vegetables, seafood, cheese, and fresh herbs, or serving it *alla carbonara* (see page 213).

choux pastry

makes 40–50 little buns

½ cup (125ml) milk
8 tbsp (100g) butter, diced
½ tsp salt
1 tsp sugar
generous 1 cup (150g) all-purpose flour
4 medium eggs
egg wash (1 egg beaten with 1 tbsp milk)

Combine the milk, ½ cup (125ml) water, the butter, salt, and sugar in a pan and set over low heat. Bring to a boil and immediately take the pan off the heat. Shower in the flour and beat the mixture with a wooden spoon until smooth.

Return the pan to medium heat for about 1 minute, stirring constantly, to dry out the paste. Tip it into a bowl.

Pipe small mounds onto a baking sheet lined with waxed paper in staggered rows, using a pastry bag fitted with a ½-inch (1-cm) tip. Brush with egg wash and lightly mark the tops with the back of a fork. Bake at 400°F (200°C) for 15 to 20 minutes, until dry and crisp, but soft inside. Cool on a wire rack.

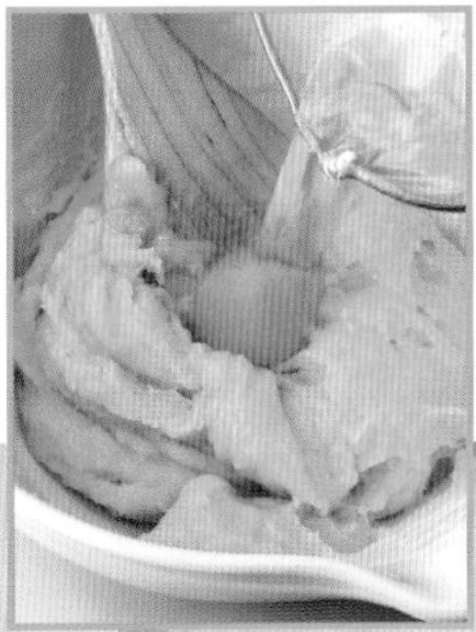

Add the eggs one by one, beating with the wooden spoon. Once they are all incorporated into the mixture, it should be smooth and shiny, and thick enough to pipe. The choux paste is now ready to use. (If you are not using it immediately, brush the surface with egg wash to prevent a crust forming.)

choux buns with coffee & drambuie mousse

serves 8–10

for the choux pastry

1/2 cup (125ml) milk
8 tbsp (100g) butter, diced
1/2 tsp salt
1 tsp sugar
generous 1 cup (150g) all-purpose flour
4 medium eggs
egg wash (1 egg beaten with 1 tbsp milk)

for the coffee mousse

generous 1/3 cup (100ml) heavy cream
1 1/2 tbsp (20g) superfine sugar
1/2 quantity (13oz/375g) crème pâtissière (see page 220), cooled
4 tbsp instant coffee powder, dissolved in 2 tbsp warm water
5 tbsp (75ml) Drambuie, or to taste

to finish

confectioners' sugar
unsweetened cocoa

Preheat the oven to 400°F (200°C). Make the choux pastry, and shape and cook the buns following the method on page 188. Let cool on a wire rack.

To make the mousse, whip the cream with the sugar to a ribbon consistency and fold into the cooled crème pâtissière, then fold in the coffee and Drambuie.

Make a small opening in the side of each choux bun with the tip of a knife. Using a pastry bag fitted with a plain 1/4-inch (5-mm) tip, pipe a generous amount of coffee mousse into each bun.

To serve, dust half the choux buns with a little confectioners' sugar and the rest with cocoa. Arrange on individual plates or a platter, allowing about 5 per person.

"These little choux buns make a lovely dessert, but I also like to serve them as a teatime treat."

gougères

makes 40–50

for the choux pastry
$^1/_2$ cup (125ml) milk
8 tbsp (100g) butter, diced
$^1/_2$ tsp salt
1 tsp sugar
generous 1 cup (150g) all-purpose flour
4 medium eggs
egg wash (1 egg beaten with 1 tbsp milk)
for the flavourings
4oz (100g) Gruyère or Comté, grated
pinch of cayenne
small pinch of freshly grated nutmeg
a little sweet paprika, to dust (optional)

Preheat the oven to 400°F (200°C). Make the choux pastry following the method on page 188. When the last egg has been incorporated and the mixture is very smooth, stir in three-quarters of the grated cheese, the cayenne, and nutmeg. Take care not to overwork the mixture.

Pipe the choux paste onto a baking sheet lined with waxed paper in staggered rows, using a pastry bag fitted with a $^1/_2$-inch (1-cm) tip. Brush with egg wash, then mark the tops lightly with the back of a fork and sprinkle with the rest of the cheese. Bake for 15 to 20 minutes, until dry and crisp on the outside, but still soft inside. Immediately transfer to a wire rack.

Serve the gougères warm, just as they are, or dusted with sweet paprika.

"These little gougères are usually offered at the end of a wine tasting in Burgundy wine cellars. They make good canapés, or you can serve them filled with Mornay sauce (see page 299) as a warm appetizer."

tart pie dough

makes 1 lb (480g)

This dough makes the perfect shell for tarts, tartlets, and quiche.

$1^3/_4$ cups all-purpose flour
9 tbsp soft butter, diced
1 medium egg
1 tsp salt
2 tsp superfine sugar

First, put the flour in a mound on a surface (preferably marble) and make a well in the middle. Put the butter, egg, salt, and sugar into the well. Using your fingertips, mix all the ingredients in the well together, then gradually draw in the flour, little by little.

Then mix until all the ingredients are almost amalgamated and the dough has a slightly sandy texture. Add about 3 tbsp (40 ml) cold water and incorporate, using your fingertips.

Knead the dough 2 or 3 times with the heel of your hand to make it completely smooth. Roll it into a ball, wrap in plastic wrap, and let rest in the refrigerator for 1 to 2 hours before using.

pâte sucrée

makes about 1lb 2oz (520g)

This sweet dough is relatively easy to work with and is perfect for blind-baked tarts and tartlets. It is made in the same way as tart dough (see left) and—like tart dough—it keeps well in the refrigerator for several days, or it can be frozen.

1³/₄ cups (250g) all-purpose flour
8 tbsp (100g) butter, diced and softened
1 cup (100g) confectioners' sugar
small pinch of salt
2 medium eggs

Put the flour on a surface (preferably marble) and make a well. Put in the butter, sugar, and salt.

Using your fingertips, mix all the ingredients in the well, then add the eggs and gradually draw in the flour, little by little, and mix well.

When everything is completely amalgamated, knead the dough 2 or 3 times with the heel of your hand to make it completely smooth, wrap in plastic wrap, and rest in the refrigerator for 1 to 2 hours before using.

lining a tart pan & baking blind

Roll out the dough on a clean, smooth surface (preferably marble) and keep dusting it with a veil of flour. Give the dough a quarter-turn each time you roll it to keep the shape as round as possible.

When you achieve the required thickness, lightly roll the dough round the rolling pin, and carefully unroll it over a flan ring or tart pan. Use your thumb and index finger to push the dough into the bottom and side of the mold.

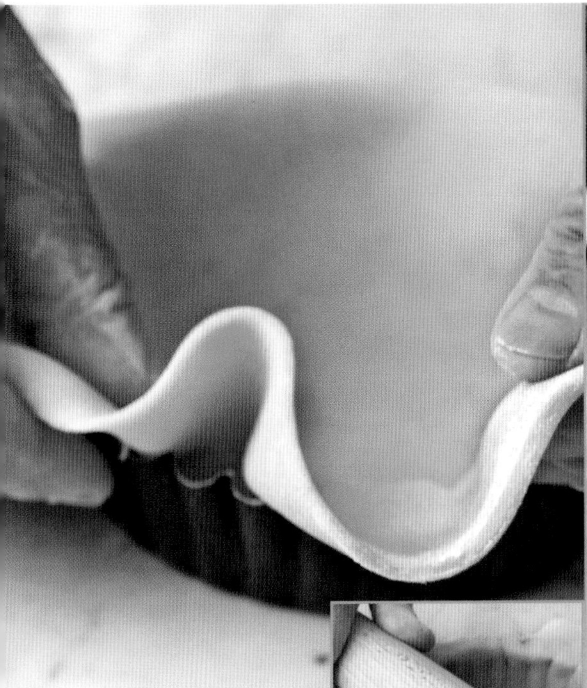

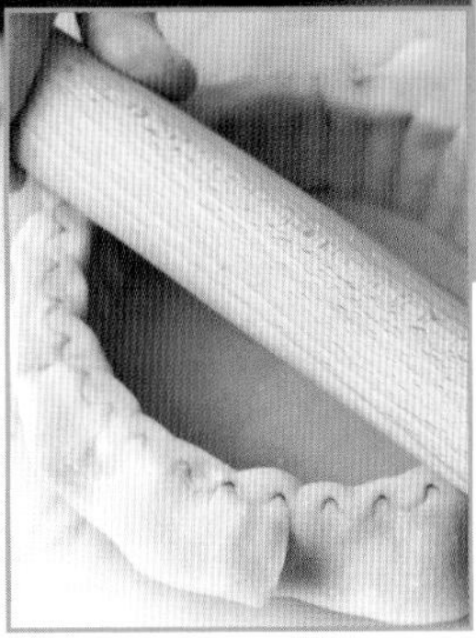

Cut off the excess dough by rolling the rolling pin across the rim of the mold, then pinch up the edges with your thumb and index finger to crimp them 1/4 inch (5mm) above the rim. Refrigerate the tart shell for at least 20 minutes before baking.

Remove the baking beans and paper and return the pastry shell to the oven for a final 10 to 15 minutes, depending on the type of pastry and its thickness.

Prick the bottom of the pastry shell in 5 or 6 places with a fork. Line it with waxed paper and fill with baking beans or dried pulses. Bake at 400–425°F (200–220°C) for about 20 minutes.

quiche lorraine

serves 8–10

"This recipe is for a large classic quiche, but you can make individual ones if you prefer, adjusting the cooking time accordingly."

3/4lb (350g) tart pie dough (see page 194)
1 1/2 tbsp (20g) butter, to grease
flour, to dust
for the filling
7oz (200g) salt pork flank, derinded and cut into small strips
1 tbsp peanut oil
7oz (200g) Gruyère or Comté, coarsely grated
3 medium eggs
6 medium egg yolks
2 1/2 cups (600ml) heavy cream
salt and freshly ground pepper
pinch of freshly grated nutmeg
2 tbsp Kirsch (optional)
to finish
1 1/2 oz (40g) Gruyère, cut into thin flakes

Grease an 8 1/2-inch (22cm) flan ring (1 1/4 inches/3cm deep) and place on a baking sheet in the refrigerator. Roll out the dough into a circle 1/8 inch (3mm) thick and use to line the flan ring (see page 196). Chill for 20 minutes. Preheat oven to 400°F (200°C).

Prick the bottom of the pastry shell, line with waxed paper and baking beans or dried pulses, and bake blind for 20 minutes. Remove the beans and paper and let cool in the ring. Increase the oven setting to 425°F (220°C).

For the filling, blanch the bacon in boiling water, refresh in cold water, drain, and dry. Heat the oil in a nonstick skillet and brown the bacon over medium heat for 1 minute; drain. Scatter in the pastry shell, then sprinkle on the grated cheese.

Lightly whisk the whole eggs, yolks, and cream in a bowl. Season with salt, pepper, and nutmeg, then add the Kirsch if using. Pour into the pastry shell and bake for 20 minutes. Lower the oven setting to 400°F (200°C) and cook for another 15 minutes. Scatter the cheese over the surface and bake for a final 5 minutes.

Immediately slide the quiche onto a wire rack, using a large spatula. Gently lift the flan ring off. Serve the quiche warm or tepid, but not piping hot.

leek flamiche

serves 8–10

"The curry adds a special something to this flan from the Champagne region of France. Perhaps surprisingly, it enhances rather than detracts from the flavor of the leeks."

$^3/_4$lb (350g) tart pie dough (see page 194)
$1^1/_2$tbsp (20g) butter, to grease
flour, to dust

for the filling
$2^1/_4$lb (1kg) leeks, trimmed, split lengthwise and well washed
$4^1/_2$tbsp (60g) butter
salt and freshly ground pepper
generous $^1/_3$ cup (100ml) heavy cream
5 medium egg yolks
1tbsp (15g) Madras curry powder (optional)

For the filling, cut the leeks into $^1/_4$-inch (5-mm) pieces. Melt the butter in a pan, add the leeks, season with a little salt and pepper, then cover and sweat gently for 20 to 30 minutes until tender, stirring occasionally. Transfer to a bowl and cool completely.

For the pastry shell, grease an $8^1/_2$-inch (22-cm) flan ring ($1^1/_4$-inches/3-cm deep), and place on a baking sheet in the refrigerator. Roll out the dough into a circle about $^1/_8$ inch (3mm) thick and use to line the flan ring (see page 196). Let rest in the refrigerator for at least 20 minutes. Preheat the oven to 400°F (200°C).

Prick the bottom of the pastry shell, line with waxed paper and baking beans or dried pulses, and bake blind for 20 minutes. Remove the beans and paper and let cool in the ring.

To make the filling, whip the cream very lightly with the egg yolks and curry powder if using, then fold in the cooled leeks. Adjust the seasoning if necessary. Pour the leek mixture into the pastry shell and bake for 40 minutes, until the top is lightly golden and the filling is cooked but still soft to the touch.

Immediately slide the flamiche onto a wire rack, using a large spatula. Gently lift the flan ring off. Serve the quiche warm or tepid, but not piping hot.

prune tartlets

serves 6

"These rustic tartlets remind me of my childhood, when they were on show in every pâtisserie and bakery window. Serve as a dessert, or at teatime."

about 1 lb 1 oz (480 g) tart dough (page 194)
2 tbsp (30 g) butter, to grease
flour, to dust
for the filling
2/3 quantity (1 lb/500 g) crème pâtissière (see page 220), freshly made, replacing half the flour with custard powder
24 very moist prunes, pitted

Grease 6 tartlet pans, 4 inches (10 cm) in diameter (1 1/4-inches/3 cm deep), and place in the refrigerator. Roll out the dough into a rectangle 1/16 inch (2–3 mm) thick. Put the tartlet pans on the surface, then lightly roll the dough round the rolling pin, and carefully unroll it over the pans. Use your thumb and index finger to push the dough into the pans to line them. Press the rolling pin onto the pans to cut off the excess dough, then lightly crimp the edges. Let the tartlets rest in the refrigerator for at least 20 minutes. Preheat the oven to 400°F (200°C).

Prick the bottom of the pastry shells in 3 or 4 places with a fork. Line the bottoms with waxed paper and fill the pans to the top with baking beans or dried pulses. Bake blind for 12 minutes, until three-quarters cooked. Remove the beans and paper and let the cases cool. Increase the oven temperature to 425°F (220°C).

Divide the hot crème pâtissière between the tartlet shells. Put 4 prunes into each one, pressing them down so that they are two-thirds immersed in the cream. Bake for 5 to 6 minutes until the tops are lightly browned. Unmold the tartlets with the aid of a small knife tip and let cool on a wire rack. Serve warm or just cold.

"Buy unwaxed lemons and wash and dry well before grating the zest. When you have squeezed all the juice from the lemons, strain it through a fine strainer to eliminate the pulp and pips."

lemon tart

serves 8–10

"The amazing freshness of my lemon tart makes it a firm favorite and it has become a classic recipe. If preferred, top the filling with meringue (see page 258) rather than glaze with sugar."

1lb 3½oz (550g) pâte sucrée (see page 195)
1½ tbsp (20g) butter, to grease
flour, to dust

for the filling
finely grated zest and juice of 4 lemons
9 medium eggs
scant 2 cups (375g) superfine sugar
1¼ cups (300ml) heavy cream, chilled
egg wash (1 egg yolk beaten with ½ tsp milk)
to glaze
2–3 tbsp brown sugar

For the tart shell, grease an 8-inch (20-cm) flan ring (1½ inches/4 cm deep) and place on a baking sheet in the refrigerator. Roll out the dough into a circle ⅛ inch (3–4 mm) thick and use to line the flan ring (see page 196). Rest in the refrigerator for 20 minutes. Preheat the oven to 400°F (200°C).

For the filling, combine the lemon zest and juice in a bowl. Lightly whisk the eggs with the sugar in another bowl. Whip the cream to a light ribbon consistency. Mix the eggs into the lemon juice, then fold this mixture into the cream. Cover and refrigerate.

Prick the bottom of the pastry shell, line with waxed paper and baking beans or dried pulses, and bake blind for 20 minutes. Remove the beans and paper and let cool for 1 to 2 minutes. Brush the inside of the pastry shell with egg wash and return to the oven for 5 minutes. Lower the oven setting to 300°F (150°C).

Give the filling a stir, then pour into the shell and bake for 1 hour 20 minutes. Cut off any excess dough from the rim. Leave the tart on the baking sheet for 20 minutes, then lift off the flan ring. Slide the tart onto a wire rack and let cool for 3 to 4 hours.

Finish the tart shortly before serving. Sprinkle the brown sugar evenly over the surface, then brown it with a cook's blowtorch or under a very hot broiler, as you would a crème brûlée. Cut the tart into slices, using a long, thin, sharp-bladed knife.

strawberry tart

serves 8

"I like to serve this delectable tart with a little red fruit coulis on the side—the perfect complement."

14oz (400g) pâte sucrée (see page 195)
$1^1/_2$tbsp (20g) butter, to grease
flour, to dust
5tbsp (75ml) heavy cream
2tbsp (30g) sugar
5oz (150g) crème pâtissière (see page 220), cooled
1lb 2oz (500g) strawberries, hulled
confectioners' sugar, to dust
red berry coulis (see page 172) (optional)

For the pastry shell, grease an 8-inch (20-cm) flan ring ($1^1/_4$ inches/3cm deep), and place on a baking sheet in the refrigerator. Roll out the dough into a circle $^1/_8$ inch (3–4mm) thick and use to line the flan ring (see page 196). Let rest in the refrigerator for at least 20 minutes. Preheat the oven to 400°F (200°C).

Prick the bottom of the pastry shell, line with waxed paper and baking beans or dried pulses, and bake blind for 20 minutes. Remove the beans and paper and return to the oven for another 10 minutes. Slide the cooked pastry shell onto a wire rack and carefully lift off the flan ring. Let cool.

For the filling, whip the cream with the sugar to a ribbon consistency, then add the crème pâtissière and mix thoroughly with a whisk. Spread evenly over the bottom of the pastry shell. Halve or quarter larger strawberries, leaving small ones whole. Arrange on top of the filling. Dust with confectioners' sugar just before serving.

Cut the delicate tart into slices, using a long, thin, sharp-bladed knife. Serve with a little fruit coulis if you like.

pasta dough

makes $^3/_4$lb (350g)

Fresh pasta will keep well-wrapped in the refrigerator for a day or two, but it is best cooked as soon as it is cut.

1 $^3/_4$ cups (250g) Italian pasta flour
1 medium egg
4 medium egg yolks
1 tbsp olive oil
pinch of salt

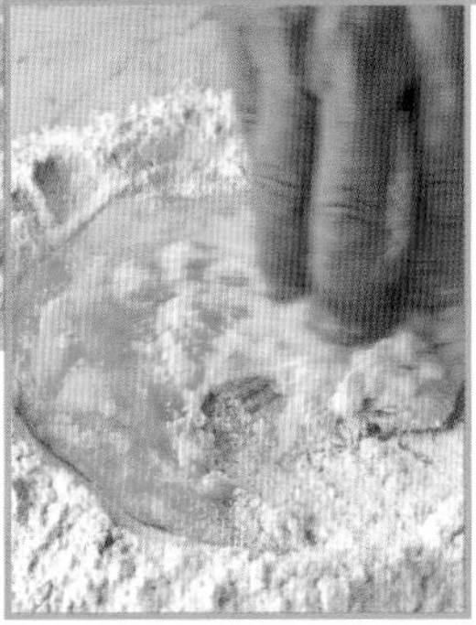

Put the flour in a mound on a clean surface (preferably marble) and make a well in the middle. Put the whole egg, egg yolks, 1 tbsp cold water, the olive oil, and salt into the well.

Using your fingertips, mix all the ingredients in the well together, then gradually draw the flour into the center, little by little.

When the dough is almost completely amalgamated, knead it 4 or 5 times with the heel of your hand, then roll it into a ball, wrap in plastic wrap, and chill for 1 hour.

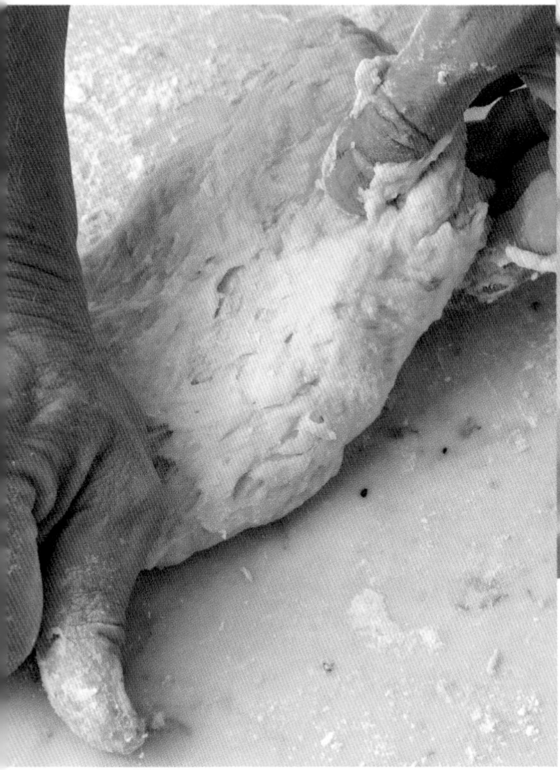

Divide the pasta dough in half; rewrap one portion. Roll the other portion through a pasta machine, starting on the widest setting. Continue to roll it through the machine repeatedly, narrowing the setting by one notch each time until the sheet of dough is $^{5}/_{8}$ inch (1.5 mm) thick. Roll it through once more to prevent shrinkage when you cut it.

Fit the appropriate cutter on the machine and cut the dough into linguine, spaghetti, or tagliatelle.

Lay the strands on a sheet of waxed paper or lightly floured parchment to aerate them and prevent tangling.

To cook the pasta, bring a large pan of lightly salted water to a boil with a few drops of olive oil added. Add the freshly cut pasta and cook for about $1\frac{1}{2}$ to 2 minutes, until it is al dente (tender, but firm to the bite). The precise cooking time is determined by the width and thickness of the pasta strands.

Tagliatelle with young spring vegetables All the following vegetables can be used to enhance fresh pasta: peas, broccoli florets, fava beans, sliced zucchini, snow peas. Simply blanch them for a few seconds and refresh, then sweat gently in a little olive oil for a minute or two. Add some snipped basil leaves and a touch of crushed garlic before tossing the vegetables with freshly cooked tagliatelle. Serve a bowl of freshly grated Parmesan on the side to complement the wonderful flavors.

Spaghetti with seafood and cherry tomatoes Steamed and shelled mussels, shelled shrimp, and sliced, lightly poached or pan-fried scallops, are exquisite mixed into freshly cooked spaghetti. I like to add some roasted cherry tomatoes (prepared in advance, as for Portuguese-style scrambled egg, see page 103), and to serve a bowl of pesto on the side (see below).

Linguine with pesto Pesto is the perfect partner for freshly made pasta. You can buy this ready made, but it's so easy to prepare, tastes far superior if it's freshly made, and the aromas will perfume your house. Simply pound 4 crushed garlic cloves with 20 basil leaves and 1/4 cup (30g) toasted pine nuts, using a mortar and pestle, then add 1 cup (100g) freshly grated Parmesan. Slowly trickle in 2/3 cup (150ml) olive oil, stirring constantly with the pestle. Once the pesto is smooth, season to taste with salt and pepper. Toss freshly cooked linguine with pesto and serve with extra grated Parmesan.

linguine alla carbonara

serves 4

"A successful carbonara depends on good pasta cooked to perfection at the last moment, a very hot serving dish and the rapid mixing in of cream and egg to create a glistening sauce, which lightly coats the pasta."

3 tbsp olive oil
7 oz (200g) onions, chopped
1 garlic clove, finely chopped
7 oz (200g) thin slices of pancetta or bacon
$^{2}/_{3}$ cup (150ml) heavy cream
4 egg yolks
scant $^{1}/_{4}$ cup snipped Italian parsley leaves
salt and freshly ground pepper
$^{3}/_{4}$lb (350g) linguine (see page 208)
$2^{1}/_{4}$oz (60g) Parmesan, freshly grated

Warm a deep serving dish in the oven at 325°F (170°C) for 10 minutes. Heat 1 tbsp olive oil in a nonstick skillet over very low heat, add the onions, and sweat gently for 2 minutes. Add the garlic, stir well, and transfer to a bowl.

In the clean, dry skillet, lightly brown the pancetta or bacon slices over medium heat. Tip onto a board and cut into $^{1}/_{2}$-inch (1-cm) pieces, then add to the onions and keep warm.

In a bowl, mix the cream, egg yolks, and parsley together, and season lightly with salt and pepper. Bring a large pan of salted water to a boil and add 1 tbsp olive oil. Add the linguine and cook for 1 to 2 minutes, until al dente, or done to your liking, then drain.

Immediately take the serving dish from oven, add the remaining 1 tbsp olive oil, and put in the pasta. Quickly pour on the cream mixture, mix rapidly with tongs, then add the bacon and onion mixture. Sprinkle with Parmesan, mix well but not too thoroughly, and serve immediately.

custards, creams & mousses

With their different textures, some creams and mousses are used as fillings or toppings for desserts and cakes, while others, like my rich chocolate & orange mousse (see page 230) and little cream caramel & coffee pots (see page 224), are stand-alone desserts. They all have something in common, though. They are light, creamy, and rather rich, so they should be served in small portions. Most can be prepared in advance and kept in the refrigerator for a day or two. Of course, crème anglaise (see page 216) is the perfect accompaniment for many desserts; I also love it with summer berries like strawberries, blueberries, and raspberries. I'm also partial to freshly cooked waffles topped with Chiboust cream (see page 221). Crème brûlée has long been a favorite of dessert lovers and I urge you to try my favorite, pistachio crème brûlée (see page 226).

crème anglaise

makes about 3 cups (750ml), 6–8 servings

generous 2 cups (500ml) milk
$^{1}/_{2}$ cup plus 2 tbsp (125g) superfine sugar
1 vanilla bean, split lengthwise
6 egg yolks

Put the milk in a pan with two-thirds of the sugar, add the vanilla bean, and bring to a boil over medium heat.

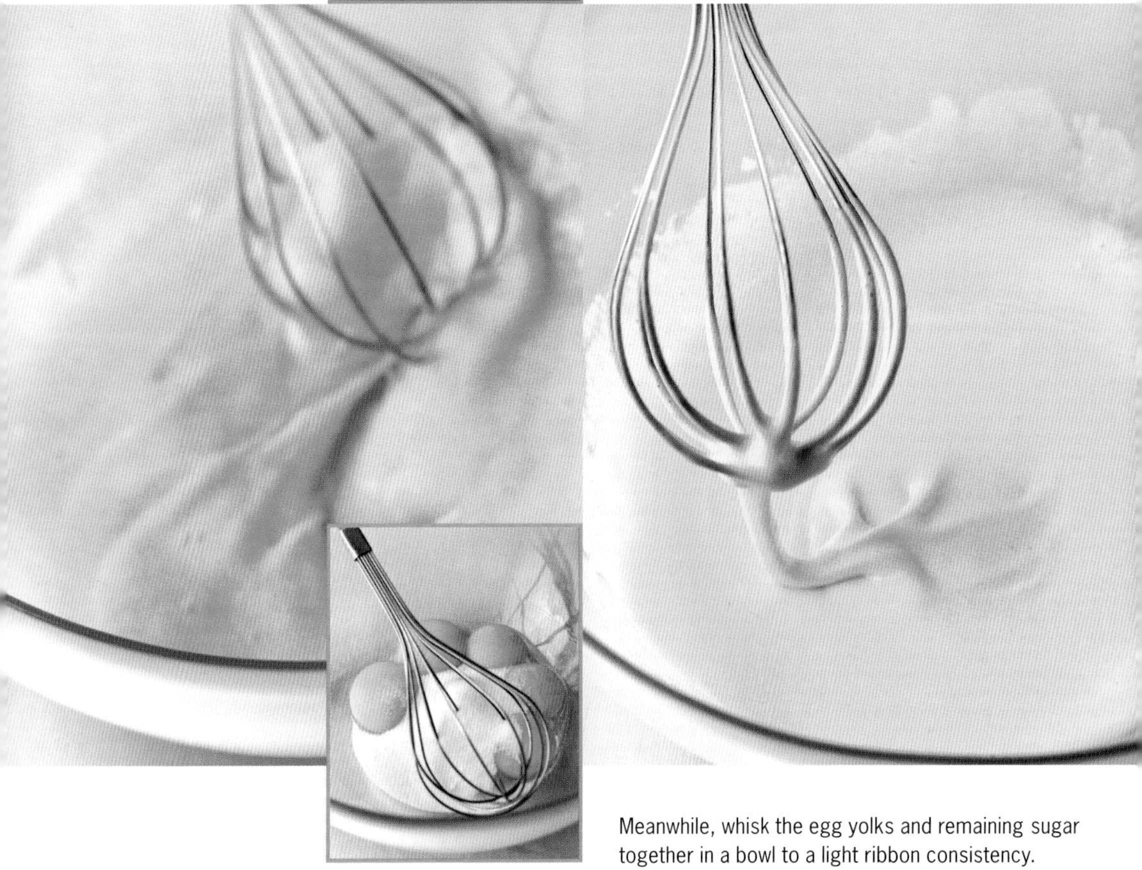

Meanwhile, whisk the egg yolks and remaining sugar together in a bowl to a light ribbon consistency.

Cook over low heat, stirring with a wooden spatula or spoon, until the custard lightly coats the back of the spatula. When you run your finger through, it should leave a clear trace. Immediately take the pan off the heat.

Unless you are serving the crème anglaise warm, pour into a bowl and let cool, stirring occasionally to prevent a skin forming. When cold, pass through a chinois or fine strainer.

Pour the boiling milk onto the egg yolks, whisking constantly, then pour the mixture back into the pan.

The custard will keep in a covered container in the refrigerator for up to 3 days.

minted crème anglaise

makes about 3 cups (750ml), 6–8 servings

"The freshness of this mint-flavored custard goes brilliantly with all berries. It is also excellent with chocolate ice cream (see page 242) or my chocolate truffle cake with candied kumquats (see page 275)."

generous 2 cups (500ml) milk
1/2 cup plus 2 tbsp (125g) superfine sugar
3oz (75g) mint leaves and stalks, chopped
6 egg yolks

Put the milk in a pan with two-thirds of the sugar and bring to a boil over medium heat. Add the mint, take the pan off the heat, cover, and let infuse for 10 minutes.

In a bowl, whisk the egg yolks and the remaining sugar to a light ribbon consistency. Bring the milk just back to a boil, then pour onto the egg yolks, whisking constantly. Pour the mixture back into the pan. Cook over low heat, stirring all the time with a wooden spatula or spoon, until the custard lightly coats the back of the spatula (see page 217).

Immediately pass the crème anglaise through a chinois or fine strainer into a bowl and set aside until completely cold, stirring occasionally with a spatula to prevent a skin forming. Once cold, cover with plastic wrap and keep in the refrigerator for up to 3 days until ready to use.

crème pâtissière

makes about 1 lb 10 oz (750 g)

"Crème pâtissière—or pastry cream—has many roles in pâtisserie, including fillings for choux buns and sweet tarts, and my Chiboust cream.'

6 egg yolks
1/2 cup plus 2 tbsp (125 g) superfine sugar
1/4 cup (40 g) all-purpose flour
generous 2 cups (500 ml) milk
1 vanilla bean, split lengthwise
a little confectioners' sugar or butter

Combine the egg yolks and one-third of the sugar in a bowl and whisk to a light ribbon consistency. Add the flour and whisk it in thoroughly.

In a pan, heat the milk with the rest of the sugar and the vanilla bean. As soon as it comes to a boil, pour it onto the egg yolk mixture, stirring as you go. Mix well, then return the mixture to the pan.

Bring to a boil over medium heat, stirring constantly with the whisk. Allow the mixture to bubble, still stirring, for 2 minutes, then tip it into a bowl.

To prevent a skin forming, dust the surface with a veil of confectioners' sugar or dot all over with little flakes of butter. Once cold, the pastry cream can be kept in the refrigerator for up to 3 days. Remove the vanilla bean before using.

NOTE For a lighter textured crème pâtissiere, I fold in 20–50% whipped cream (ie 2/3–1 3/4 cups/150–300 ml). Or for a rich velvety texture, I incorporate 10% whipped softened butter (ie 3 oz/75 g).

chiboust cream

makes about 2½lb (1.2kg)

"This wonderfully rich, velvety cream is perfect for serving with waffles, filling crêpes and topping fruit tarts to make them even more tempting."

for the pastry cream

6 egg yolks
scant ½ cup (80g) sugar
1 heaping tbsp (30g) custard powder
1½ cups (350ml) milk
1 vanilla bean, split lengthwise
a little confectioners' sugar, to dust

for the Italian meringue

generous 1¾ cups (360g) superfine sugar
1oz (30g) liquid glucose (optional)
6 egg whites

For the pastry cream, combine the egg yolks and one-third of the sugar in a bowl and whisk to a light ribbon consistency. Add the custard powder and whisk thoroughly. Heat the milk with the rest of the sugar and the vanilla bean. As soon as it comes to a boil, pour it onto the egg yolk mixture, stirring all the time.

Return the mixture to the pan and bring to a boil over medium heat, stirring with the whisk. Allow to bubble, still stirring, for 2 minutes, then tip it into a bowl. Dust the surface with confectioners' sugar to prevent a skin forming.

Make the Italian meringue (following the step-by-step instructions on page 256).

Remove the vanilla bean from the pastry cream. Using a whisk, stir in one-third of the Italian meringue, then delicately fold in the rest using a spatula to make a smooth cream. Use the Chiboust cream straightaway, or see note (below).

NOTE For a firmer consistency, or to keep the cream for a few hours after making it, soak 2 sheets of leaf gelatin in cold water for a few minutes, then drain well and fold them into the hot pastry cream as soon as you have made it, stirring until melted.

blackberry ripple mousse

serves 6

$^3/_4$lb (350g) blackberries, plus extra to serve (optional)
$^2/_3$ cup (130g) superfine sugar
juice of 1 lemon
generous $^1/_3$ cup (100ml) heavy cream
$^1/_3$ quantity (9oz/250g) crème pâtissière (see page 220), cooled
2 egg whites

Put the blackberries in a pan with $^1/_2$ cup (100g) sugar and heat very gently, stirring with a wooden spoon from time to time. When the mixture comes to a simmer, cook gently for another 10 minutes. Transfer to a blender or food processor and whiz to a purée, then strain through a cheesecloth-lined strainer into a bowl. Let this coulis cool, stirring occasionally to prevent a skin forming. When cold, stir in the lemon juice.

Whip the cream to a ribbon consistency, then fold into the cooled crème pâtissière.

Whisk the egg whites in a clean bowl to a thick foam, then add the remaining sugar and whisk to soft peaks. Gently fold in the pastry cream mixture, without overworking.

Very delicately mix in the cold blackberry coulis to create a ripple effect. Divide the mousse between 6 glass dishes and refrigerate for 2 to 3 hours before serving.

Serve the mousse on its own, or with extra berries.

"You may need to adjust the quantity of sugar for cooking the blackberries according to how ripe they are. This mousse is equally delicious made with flavorful strawberries or raspberries."

little cream caramel & coffee pots

serves 6

"Soft as velvet, creamy, satisfyingly long in the mouth, and full of flavor—I can happily eat two of these unctuous creams..."

scant 1 cup (180g) superfine sugar
generous 1 cup (250ml) milk
generous 1/3 cup (100ml) heavy cream
1 tbsp (15g) instant coffee granules or powder
3 eggs
2 egg yolks
1/4 cup (40g) brown sugar (optional)

Have ready 6 little ovenproof pots, about 2 inches (5cm) in diameter and 2 1/2 inches (6cm) deep. Put 1/2 cup (100g) superfine sugar in a small heavy pan and melt over medium heat, stirring until it is liquid and turns a pale caramel color. Immediately pour into the pots and rotate them to coat the insides with the hot caramel, using a cloth to protect your hands. Let cool completely. Preheat the oven to 250°F (120°C).

Combine the milk, cream, coffee, and 1/4 cup (50g) sugar in a pan and gently bring to a boil, stirring to dissolve the coffee. Whisk the eggs, yolks and remaining 1/8 cup (30g) sugar in a bowl for 1 minute. Pour the boiling milk onto the egg mixture, whisking.

Divide the mixture between the caramel-lined pots. Stand them in a deep ovenproof dish lined with waxed paper and pour in hot (not boiling) water to come about halfway up the sides. Cook in the oven for 45 minutes, or until a thin-bladed knife tip inserted into the center of a custard comes out clean. If necessary, cook for an extra 5 to 10 minutes. Place the pots on a wire rack to cool, then chill for several hours.

I like to caramelize the creams before serving. To do this, sprinkle the tops with the brown sugar and caramelize with a cook's blowtorch for a few seconds. If you prefer, simply unmold the creams onto plates—the caramel will run out as you do so.

pistachio crème brûlée

serves 6–8

"If you can't find pistachio paste, you can make your own by pounding freshly skinned pistachios in a mortar to make a smooth paste."

generous 2 cups (500ml) milk
generous 2 cups (500ml) heavy cream
2¼oz (60g) pistachio paste
¾ cup (150g) superfine sugar
7oz (200g) egg yolks (about 10)
⅓ cup (70g) raw brown sugar

Preheat the oven to 250°F (120°C). To make the custard, heat the milk, cream, pistachio paste, and scant ½ cup (90g) superfine sugar in a pan, whisking until well blended, then slowly bring to a boil. Meanwhile, in a bowl, lightly whisk the egg yolks with the remaining superfine sugar. As soon as the milk mixture comes to a boil, gradually pour it onto the egg mixture, whisking all the time.

Ladle the custard into 6-inch (15-cm) gratin dishes and place on a baking sheet. Cook in the oven for 30 minutes, or until just set. Transfer the dishes to a wire rack and leave until the custards are cold, then chill until ready to serve.

Just before serving, sprinkle the tops with the raw brown sugar and caramelize with a cook's blowtorch, or under a very hot broiler, to make a thin, pale nut-brown topping. Serve immediately.

rich chocolate and orange mousse

serves 4

"Fresh orange segments and toasted brioche complement this rich mousse perfectly."

5oz (150g) semisweet chocolate (55–70% cocoa solids), chopped into small pieces
1 tbsp superfine sugar
2 egg yolks
2/3 cup (150ml) heavy cream
scant 1/3 cup (30g) confectioners' sugar

to decorate
1 orange, washed
1/2 cup (100g) superfine sugar

First prepare the decoration. Finely pare the zest from the orange into fine strips, using a zester. Place in a pan, cover with cold water, and bring to a boil over medium heat. Refresh and drain, then repeat this process twice more. Put the zests in a small pan with generous 1/3 cup (100ml) water and the sugar. Bring to a boil and bubble for 1 minute, then let the zests cool in the syrup. When cold, drain and set aside.

To make the chocolate mousse, place the chocolate in a bowl set over a pan of gently simmering water to melt (making sure the bowl isn't in direct contact with the water). Dissolve the sugar in 1 tbsp water in a small pan over low heat, bring to the boil, then take off the heat and let cool. When the chocolate has melted, take the bowl off the heat. Mix the sugar syrup with the egg yolks and 2 tbsp warm water, then mix into the melted chocolate.

In another bowl, whip the cream with the confectioners' sugar to a ribbon consistency, then delicately fold into the mousse mixture, without overworking it.

Pour one-third of the mousse mixture into 4 glasses or glass dishes, about 2 1/2 inches (6cm) in diameter, or 4 large ramekins. Scatter one-third of the zests on top. Repeat these layers twice, finishing with a layer of mousse sprinkled with orange zest. Chill for an hour before serving. If chilled for longer, remove 30 minutes before serving.

illustrated on previous page

caramel mousse

serves 8–10

"Serve this rich, creamy mousse in lightly chilled glasses, but don't chill the mousse before serving. Thin slices of Genoese sponge (see page 268) make an excellent accompaniment."

for the caramel cream
1$^{3}/_{4}$ cups (400ml) whipping cream
$^{2}/_{3}$ cup (150ml) liquid glucose
1 cup (200g) superfine sugar
4 tbsp (50g) butter, diced

for the pâte à bombe
scant $^{1}/_{3}$ cup (60g) superfine sugar
1oz (30g) liquid glucose
6 egg yolks
3 sheets of leaf gelatin, soaked in cold water
scant 1 cup (220ml) whipping cream

To make the caramel cream, heat the cream and glucose in a pan until boiling. Meanwhile, put the sugar in a small heavy pan and melt it gently, stirring with a wooden spoon until it turns pale golden. Take the pan off the heat, immediately pour on the cream mixture, then return to low heat and gently bring back to a boil. Bubble for 2 minutes, then turn off the heat and whisk in the butter. Pass the caramel cream through a chinois or fine strainer and let cool (to about 75°F/24°C).

For the pâte à bombe, put 5$^{1}/_{2}$ tbsp (80ml) water, the sugar, and glucose in a heavy pan and dissolve over low heat, brushing any crystals down the side of the pan with a pastry brush dipped in cold water. Let the syrup bubble for 2 to 3 minutes until light caramel at the edge. Put the egg yolks in a bowl and whisk in the syrup in a thin stream. Stand over a pan of boiling water and whisk for 5 minutes, until it reaches 158°F (70°C). Take off the pan and carry on whisking until it is about 75°F (24°C). Squeeze excess water from the gelatin then dissolve in 2 tbsp hot water and fold into the bombe mixture.

In another bowl, whip the cream to a ribbon consistency. When the caramel cream and the bombe mixture are both about the same temperature, delicately fold them together with the whisk, then fold in the whipped cream. The mousse is now ready to serve.

NOTE If liquid glucose is unobtainable, use light corn syrup instead.

chilled lemon soufflé

serves 8–10

"This is equally delicious served chilled or iced—the choice is yours."

1 tbsp peanut oil
6 medium eggs, separated
2/3 cup (130g) superfine sugar
finely grated zest and juice of 4 lemons
2 sheets of leaf gelatin, soaked in cold water
generous 2 cups (500ml) heavy cream

to decorate
2 lemons, washed
1 cup (200g) sugar
1/4 cup (20g) slivered almonds, lightly toasted

First prepare a soufflé dish, 5 inches (13cm) in diameter and 3 1/4 inches (8cm) high. Wrap a triple thick band of waxed paper around the dish, wide enough to extend 2 1/2–3 1/4 inches (6–8cm) above the rim. Secure with tape and string. Brush the exposed inside paper with oil. Place in the refrigerator.

Whisk the egg yolks, about 3/8 cup (80g) sugar and the lemon zest together in a bowl until the mixture is thick enough to leave a light trail when you lift the whisk. Warm the lemon juice, squeeze out excess water from the gelatin leaves, then dissolve them in the lemon juice. Whisk into the egg yolk mixture and whisk for 1 minute. In another bowl, whip the cream to a ribbon consistency, then fold into the lemon mixture. Whisk the egg whites to a thick foam, then whisk in the remaining 1/4 cup (50g) sugar to soft peaks. Fold into the soufflé mixture and immediately spoon it into the dish to come 1 1/2–2 inches (4–5cm) above the rim. Smooth the surface with the back of a spoon. Chill the soufflé for 6 to 8 hours, or freeze for 3 to 4 hours before serving.

For the decoration, slice the lemons into thin circles, halve the slices, and place in a pan with scant 1 cup (200ml) water and the sugar. Bring to a boil and bubble gently for 2 minutes. Let cool; keep the lemon slices in the syrup until ready to use.

To serve, remove the paper collar from the soufflé. Sprinkle the almonds over the center and arrange the lemon slices around them. Serve immediately.

lemon curd

makes $1^1/4$lb (550g)

"Although we think of a fruit curd as a preserve, it is more like a rich custard, in which the fruit juice takes the place of milk, and butter adds richness. I use this lemon curd to fill tiny pâte sucrée tartlets (see page 195), and serve them as petits fours."

generous $1^1/2$ sticks (200g) butter, diced
1 cup (200g) superfine sugar
grated zest and juice of 3 lemons
4 egg yolks

Put the butter, sugar, lemon zest, and juice into a heatproof bowl. Stand the bowl over a pan of simmering water (making sure the bottom of the bowl isn't in direct contact with the water). The butter will begin to melt after a few minutes. Whisk the mixture until it is completely smooth.

Add the egg yolks and whisk vigorously for about 10 minutes, until the mixture begins to thicken. Pour the lemon curd into a jar or small ramekins, cover with plastic wrap, and leave in the refrigerator.

Serve this divinely rich lemon curd straight from the jar or ramekins. Spread it like butter on toasted brioche or scones for a real treat.

"For orange curd, substitute the lemons with 2 oranges and boil the juice to reduce by one-third before you start. I adore orange curd spread on crêpes (see page 168)."

ice creams

Based on eggs, milk, sugar, and a little cream, homemade ice cream is quick and easy to make, and tastes infinitely better than any bought variety. Ice creams originated in China and were introduced into Europe by the Italians in the 17th century. Their popularity soon spread. An ice-cream maker is a good investment, especially if you have children. Made with fresh ingredients, without artificial colorings or preservatives, homemade ice cream is much healthier than its commercial equivalent. To enjoy the ice cream at its best, eat it soon after churning. Ice creams can be served alone or with meringues, cookies, or petits fours. Red berry coulis is delicious poured over vanilla ice cream, as is chocolate sauce on banana ice cream. And do try my Camembert ice cream (see page 253). Served with graham crackers, it's a delight.

vanilla ice cream **serves 8**

Adding heavy cream makes this classic ice cream extra rich and creamy, but you can make it without.

1 quantity crème anglaise (see page 216)
$^{1}/_{3}$ cup (100ml) heavy cream (optional)

When the crème anglaise is ready, pour it into a stainless steel or glass bowl. Stand the bottom of the bowl on ice to hasten the cooling, and stir with a spatula from time to time to prevent a skin forming. When it is cold, remove the vanilla bean, then pour into an ice-cream maker and start churning.

After about 10 minutes, the ice cream should be half-frozen. If you are using the cream, add it in a steady stream while the machine is still running.

The texture of ice cream is best if it is served shortly after churning.

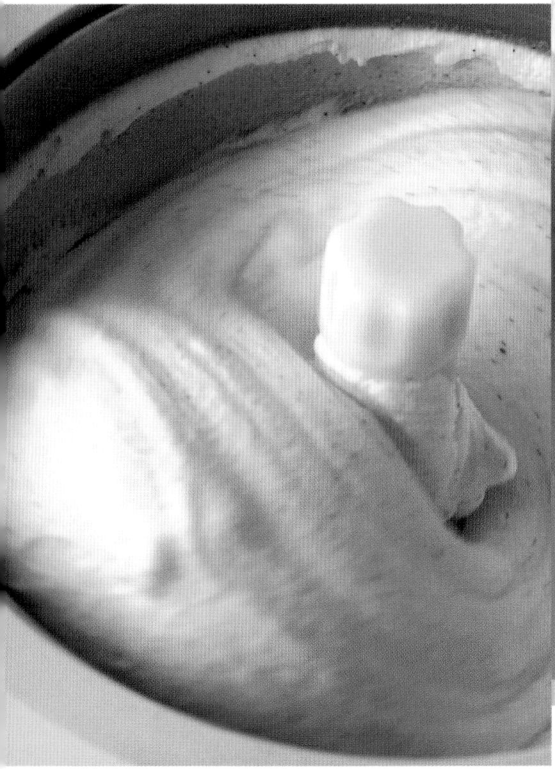

Carry on churning for 10 to 15 minutes, until the ice cream has set. It should be firm but still creamy.

Transfer the ice cream to a chilled freezer-proof container and keep it in the freezer until ready to serve.

cinnamon ice cream

serves 8

"Everyone adores this wonderful ice cream when they taste it. I find it goes particularly well with baked apples."

1 quantity crème anglaise (see page 216), infused with a ¾oz (20g) cinnamon stick, lightly broken, instead of vanilla
⅓ cup (100ml) heavy cream (optional)
to serve (optional)
8 Rome Beauty, McIntosh or other baking apples
superfine sugar, to sprinkle
8 little bits of butter

Make the ice cream following the method on page 238, leaving the cinnamon in the mixture until you are ready to churn it. Strain the infused mixture through a fine strainer or cheesecloth into the ice-cream maker and churn until the ice cream is the correct consistency.

If serving the ice cream with baked apples, use an apple corer to remove the cores, then make an incision with a knife tip all round the circumference of each apple. Stand them in a deep ovenproof dish, sprinkle with a little sugar, and put a little bit of butter on each apple. Pour a little water into the dish and bake at 350°F (180°C) for 40 minutes. Let cool slightly.

Once the apples are just warm, put them on individual plates, top them with a large scoop of cinnamon ice cream, and serve.

chocolate ice cream

serves 6

"I like to serve this ice cream scooped into coffee meringue shells (see page 260) but, of course, it will complement many desserts and is delicious served on its own."

$^2/_3$ cup (150ml) milk
$^2/_3$ cup (150ml) heavy cream
scant $^1/_2$ cup (80g) superfine sugar
3 egg yolks
4oz (100g) semisweet chocolate (55–70% cocoa solids), cut into small pieces

Put the milk and cream in a pan with two-thirds of the sugar and bring to a boil over medium heat. Meanwhile, whisk the egg yolks and the remaining sugar together in a bowl to a light ribbon consistency. Pour the boiling milk onto the egg yolks, whisking constantly, then pour the mixture back into the pan.

Cook over low heat, stirring with a wooden spatula or spoon, until the custard lightly coats the back of the spatula. When you run your finger through, it should leave a clear trace (see page 217). Immediately take the pan off the heat, add the pieces of chocolate, and stir with a whisk until melted.

Pour the mixture into a bowl and let cool over ice, stirring occasionally to prevent a skin forming. When it is cold, pass through a fine strainer into the ice-cream maker, then churn it for 20 to 25 minutes, following the method on page 238, until the ice cream is firm but still creamy.

tea ice cream

serves 8

"The only teas I use for making ice cream are Earl Grey and jasmine, but you might like to experiment with other flavors. I like to serve this ice cream with my raspberry macaroons (see page 266)."

1 quantity crème anglaise (see page 216), infused with 2oz (50g) loose-leaf Earl Grey or jasmine tea, instead of vanilla (see note)
generous 1/3 cup (100ml) heavy cream (optional)

Make the ice cream following the method on page 238, leaving the tea in the mixture until you churn it. Strain the infused mixture through a strainer or cheesecloth into the ice-cream maker and churn until the ice cream is the correct consistency.

Serve scooped into individual dishes, with dessert cookies or a petit fours, such as raspberry macaroons.

NOTE For optimum flavor, add the tea leaves to the milk just before it reaches a boil.

preserved ginger ice cream

serves 8

"Even those who don't like ginger will be tempted by this ice cream. It's amazing how ice cream can elevate ingredients to a different level."

1 quantity crème anglaise (see page 216), made without vanilla
3oz (75g) preserved ginger in syrup, drained and chopped
$^{1}/_{4}$ cup (30g) dry unsweetened coconut

Pour the hot crème anglaise into a food processor, add the chopped ginger, and whiz for 1 minute, then strain through a chinois or fine strainer into a bowl. Stand the bottom of the bowl on ice to hasten the cooling, and stir with a spatula from time to time to prevent a skin forming on the surface.

Mix in the dry unsweetened coconut, then pour the mixture into the ice-cream maker. Churn for 20 to 25 minutes, following the method on page 238, until the ice cream is firm but still creamy. Serve scooped into dishes or onto small plates.

'I like to serve this ice cream on small plates with wafer-thin slices of fresh pineapple.'

illustrated on previous page

chestnut ice cream

serves 8

"This is one of my favorite ice creams. I sometimes serve it with a pitcher of simple chocolate sauce—just warm melted semisweet chocolate with a dash of milk added."

1/4 cup (50ml) milk
5oz (150g) sweetened chestnut purée
1/2 cup (100g) superfine sugar
6 egg yolks
2 tbsp (30ml) rum (optional)
1/3 cup (100ml) heavy cream
4oz (100g) marrons glaçés or marrons in syrup (optional)

Put the milk, chestnut purée, and two-thirds of the sugar in a pan and bring to a boil over medium heat. Meanwhile, whisk the egg yolks and the remaining sugar together in a bowl to a light ribbon consistency. Pour the boiling milk onto the egg yolks, whisking constantly, then pour the mixture back into the pan.

Cook over low heat, stirring with a wooden spatula or spoon, until the custard lightly coats the back of the spatula. When you run your finger through, it should leave a clear trace (see page 217). Immediately take the pan off the heat and pour into a bowl. Add the rum if desired and let cool over ice, stirring occasionally to prevent a skin forming.

When cold, pass the mixture through a chinois or fine strainer into the ice-cream maker and churn for 20 to 25 minutes following the method on page 238 and adding the cream as directed. The ice cream is ready when it is firm but still creamy.

Serve scoops of ice cream piled into shallow bowls and topped with small pieces of marrons glaçés if you like.

banana & golden raisin ice cream

serves 8

"This ice cream is superb served with warm banana halves, quickly sautéed in butter, and drizzled with a ribbon of apricot glaze."

2 tbsp (30g) butter
$^1/_4$ cup (50g) superfine sugar
1 ripe banana, about $6^1/_2$oz (180g), sliced
juice of 1 lemon
1 quantity crème anglaise (see page 216), made with 2 tbsp (25g) sugar and without vanilla
$^1/_3$ cup (60g) golden raisins

Heat the butter in a skillet, add the sugar, then the banana slices, and cook over medium heat for 1 to 2 minutes, until the banana is lightly caramelized. Pour on the lemon juice, then mix the banana into the hot crème anglaise, stirring with a spatula.

Transfer the mixture to a blender and whiz for 1 minute, then pass through a fine strainer into a bowl. Stand over ice to hasten the cooling, and stir with a spatula from time to time to prevent a skin forming. Meanwhile, blanch the golden raisins in boiling water for 1 minute, then remove and refresh in cold water, drain, and set aside.

Pour the banana mixture into an ice-cream maker and churn for 20 to 25 minutes, following the method on page 238, until the ice cream is firm but still creamy. Stir in the golden raisins a minute or two before removing the ice cream from the machine.

Scoop the ice cream into dishes and serve with caramelized banana halves if you like.

camembert ice cream

serves 8

"I first created this original ice cream in the 1960s. I like to serve it as a palate-cleanser, accompanied by small radishes, a few tender celery leaves, and some crackers for cheese."

1/4 cup (50ml) milk
6 egg yolks
2 tbsp (25g) superfine sugar
pinch of salt
1 fine ripe Camembert, about 10oz (300g)
small pinch of cayenne
8 drops of Tabasco

Bring the milk to a boil in a pan. Meanwhile, in a bowl, whisk the egg yolks with the sugar and salt to a light ribbon consistency. Pour the boiling milk onto the egg yolks, whisking constantly, then pour the mixture back into the pan.

Cook over low heat, stirring with a wooden spatula, until the custard lightly coats the back of the spatula. When you run your finger through, it should leave a clear trace (see page 217). Immediately take the pan off the heat and pour the custard into a bowl.

Cut off the minimum of crust from the Camembert, then cut the cheese into thin slivers over the custard. Mix well with a whisk until the cheese has melted, then add the cayenne and Tabasco.

Stand the bottom of the bowl on ice to hasten the cooling, and stir with a spatula from time to time to prevent a skin forming. Pour the mixture into an ice-cream maker and churn for 20 to 25 minutes, following the method on page 238, until the ice cream is firm but still creamy. Serve in individual bowls.

meringues & sponges

Meringues are crunchy, sponges are soft and mellow, but both are light and delicious. They form the basis of many desserts and go well with ice creams, coulis, creams, and mousses. French meringues are very quick and easy to make—all you need is some egg whites and a little sugar—and they freeze well. The phenomenon of whisking egg whites into snowy peaks is intriguing. Whisking traps air bubbles inside the whites, which inflate to 6 to 8 times their original volume. Pavlova (see page 263) is one of my favorite meringue desserts. Versatile Genoese sponge takes only 20 minutes to make and can be kept wrapped in plastic wrap for up to 3 days in the refrigerator, or frozen. Eat it with fruit salad, ice cream, or on its own. Genoese is also the base for my chocolate truffle cake (see page 275) and raspberry roulade (see page 272).

italian meringue

makes 1lb 5oz (600g)

$1^3/_4$ cups (360g) superfine sugar
1oz (30g) liquid glucose (optional)
6 medium egg whites

Pour about 5 tbsp (80 ml) water into a pan, add the sugar, and glucose if using, and set over medium heat. Bring to a boil, stirring occasionally and brushing down crystals that form on side of the pan, with a pastry brush moistened with water. Increase the heat and place a sugar thermometer in the boiling syrup to register when it reaches 230°F (110°C).

Still keeping an eye on the syrup, beat the egg whites until they hold peaks, either by hand or with an electric mixer. Stop cooking the syrup the moment it reaches 250°F (121°C). Take off the heat and let the bubbling subside for 30 seconds. Pour the syrup onto the beaten egg whites in a thin, steady stream, whisking at low speed with the mixer or by hand until very firm.

A sugar thermometer is essential for preparing this meringue.

When all the syrup has been absorbed, continue to beat at low speed for 15 minutes, until the meringue is almost cold (86–95°F/30–35°C). It is now ready to use (see overleaf).

The meringue can be kept in a container in the refrigerator for up to 48 hours before use.

uses for italian meringue

Lemon meringue tart Follow the recipe for my classic lemon tart (see page 205), omitting the brown sugar glaze. Instead, pipe 1/3 quantity (9oz/250g) Italian meringue (see page 256) over the top of the tart to cover the filling, using a pastry bag fitted with a fluted tip. Wave a cook's blowtorch over the surface until the meringue is lightly tinged browned, or place under a very hot broiler for a few seconds.

Baked Alaska Line a soufflé dish or heatproof salad bowl with food-safe plastic wrap and layer two different ice creams, such as chocolate (see page 242) and vanilla (see page 238) in the dish. Place in the freezer for several hours to harden. Make a Genoese sponge (see page 268) 1 1/2–2 inches (4–5cm) wider than the bottom of the dish. Using a serrated knife, slice off the top 1/2–3/4 inch (1–2cm) of the sponge to make a base for the baked Alaska.

Dip the bottom of the dish into hot water for about 20 seconds, then unmold the ice cream and invert it onto the sponge base. Using a pastry bag fitted with a large fluted tip, pipe 1/2 quantity Italian meringue (see page 256) all over the ice cream to cover it completely. Place under a hot broiler for a few seconds to lightly brown the meringue, or do this with a cook's blowtorch.

Buttercream Measure an equal weight of butter to Italian meringue, cut it into small pieces and soften at room temperature for a few hours. When the meringue has cooled to 86–95°F (30–35°C) (at which point it is ready to use), add the butter, whisking vigorously until smooth. If you wish, flavor the buttercream with a little pistachio paste, cocoa powder, vanilla extract, or coffee essence.

Use this light buttercream as a filling for sponge cakes (see page 268) or choux buns (see page 188).

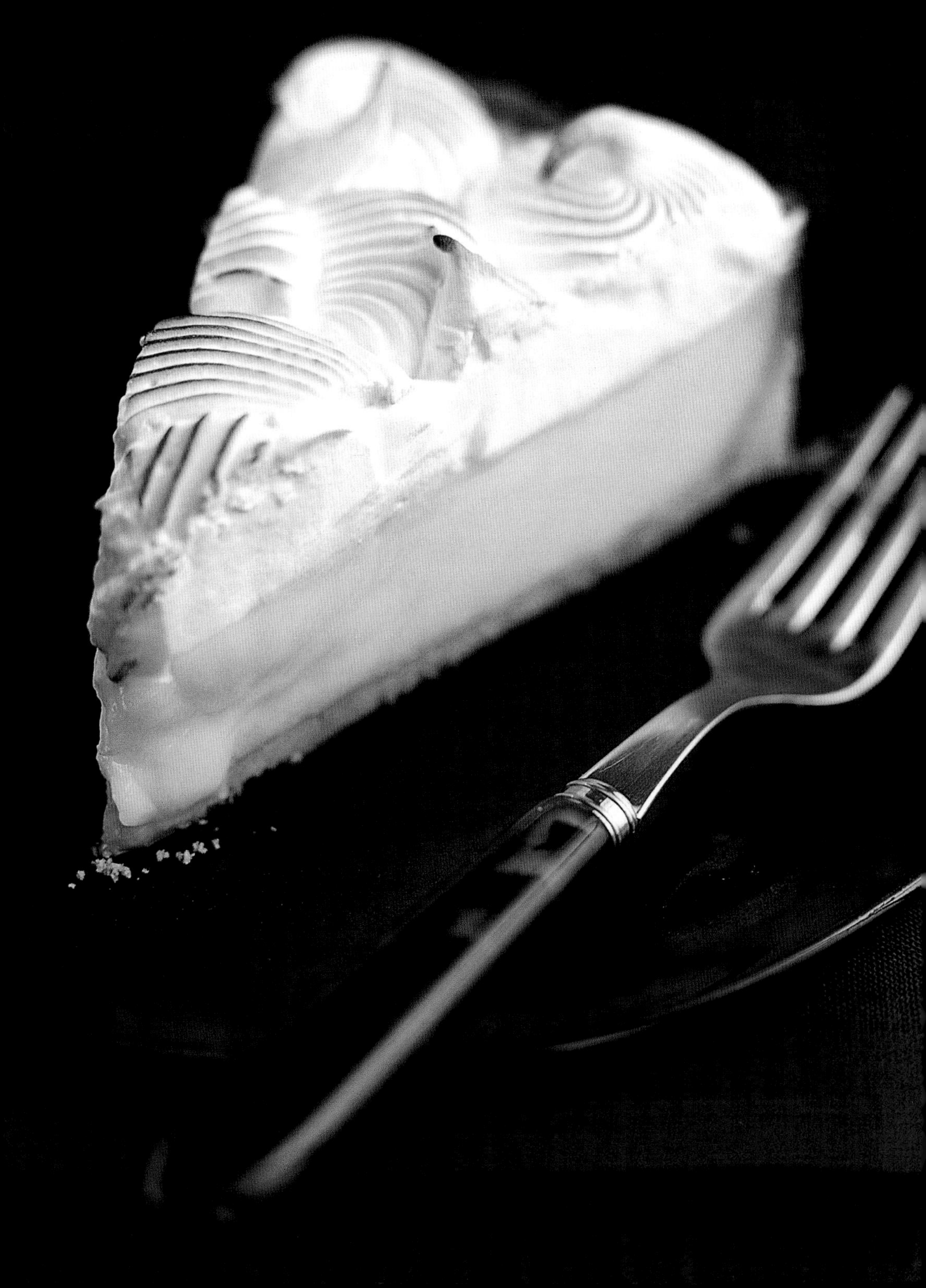

french meringues

makes $^3/_4$lb (350g), serves 6–8

"My favorite flavorings for these meringues are coffee, lemon, and vanilla. I sometimes dip the base of the coffee meringues in melted chocolate ... naughty but nice."

4 medium egg whites
$^1/_2$ cup plus 2 tbsp (125g) superfine sugar
$1^1/_4$ cups (125g) confectioners' sugar, sifted
for the flavorings (optional)
coffee extract
raspberry or lemon extract
unsweetened cocoa

In a bowl, beat the egg whites with a balloon whisk until they form soft peaks. Still whisking constantly, shower in the superfine sugar, a little at a time, and continue to whisk for about 10 minutes, until the mixture is smooth and shiny, and holds firm points on the whisk when you lift it out of the mixture. Shower in the confectioners' sugar and fold it in with a spatula. (Alternatively, you can use an electric mixer.)

The meringue is now ready to make plain meringues. For flavored meringues, divide between 2 or 3 bowls and flavor as you wish: stir in a few drops of coffee extract, or a few drops of raspberry or lemon extract, or $^1/_2$–1 tsp cocoa.

Preheat the oven to 225°F (110°C). Using a tablespoon, shape the meringue into large quenelles and place them on a baking sheet lined with parchment paper, or pipe them using a plain or fluted tip if you prefer. Cook in the oven for $1^1/_4$ hours for small meringues, or allow an extra 5 to 10 minutes for larger ones.

When the meringues are ready, switch off the oven and let them cool inside for several hours. I like to serve these meringues as petits fours, or with ice cream. They keep well for several days in an airtight container stored in a dry place.

NOTE To make meringue nests, spoon the meringue into ovals, $3^1/_2$ x$1^1/_2$ inches (8 x 4cm), and make a hollow in the middle with the back of a spoon dipped in water. Bake as above, allowing $1^1/_2$ hours.

"This is undoubtedly one of the finest desserts in the world. My Australian wife, Robyn, and Bette, her mother, make the best pavlovas I have ever tasted. The fruits you use must be ripe, very sweet, and full of flavor."

pavlova with berries, mango & passion fruit

serves 8

1 quantity French meringue (see page 260)
1 mango
$^2/_3$ cup (100g) strawberries or wild strawberries
$^2/_3$ cup (100g) raspberries
$^3/_4$ cup (100g) red currants
$^2/_3$ cup (100g) blackberries
$^2/_3$ cup (100g) blueberries
$1^3/_4$ cups (400ml) heavy cream
1 tbsp rose water (optional)
4 passion fruit, halved
superfine or confectioners' sugar, to dust

Preheat the oven to 300°F (150°C). Line a baking sheet with parchment paper and spread the meringue into a rough disk, $8^1/_2$ inches (22 cm) in diameter, 2 inches (5 cm) high. Cook in the oven for 30 minutes, then lower the setting to 250°F (120°C) and cook for another 45 minutes.

Switch off the oven and leave the pavlova inside to cool for at least 6 to 8 hours, or preferably overnight. It should then be half-cooked in the middle, crisp on the outside, and the edges should be slightly cracked.

Peel and thinly slice the mango off the seed. Rinse the berries in cold water if necessary, hull or destalk them, and place on paper towels to dry.

Carefully peel off the parchment and place the pavlova on a flat serving plate. Whip the cream with the rose water to a very light ribbon consistency, then spoon on top of the pavlova. Scatter the fruits over the surface, and then spoon the passion fruit pulp and seeds over the top. Dust with sugar and serve at once.

salzburger nockerl

serves 4

"A cross between a meringue and a soufflé, this has a melting texture and a vanilla aroma—perfect with strawberries and ice cream."

$1\frac{1}{2}$ tbsp (20g) butter, to grease
6 egg yolks
$\frac{3}{4}$ cup (75g) confectioner's sugar, plus extra to dust
2 vanilla beans, split
4 medium egg whites
$\frac{1}{2}$ cup (100g) superfine sugar

to serve

14oz (400g) strawberries

Preheat the oven to 350°F (180°C) and butter a shallow oval ovenproof dish, measuring about 12 x 8 inches (30 x 20cm). Put the egg yolks and confectioners' sugar into a small bowl. Scrape out the seeds from the vanilla bean and add them to the bowl, then whisk the mixture to a ribbon consistency.

In a separate bowl, whisk the egg whites to a thick foam, then add the superfine sugar and whisk until firm and smooth. Delicately fold half the egg whites into the yolk mixture with a skimmer or slotted spoon, then gently fold in the rest.

Immediately, spoon the meringue mixture into the buttered dish, heaping it into 2 or 3 little mounds, then smooth it with a knife. Bake at once in the oven for 3 to 4 minutes, just long enough to half-cook the meringue and to color it lightly.

As soon as the meringue comes out of the oven, dust with confectioners' sugar and arrange the strawberries around the edge. Serve immediately.

"I sometimes top warm vanilla-flavored apple compote with this meringue mixture and bake it briefly as above ... give it a try."

floating islands

serves 4

4 cups (1 liter) milk
scant 1 cup (190g) superfine sugar
6 medium egg whites
peanut oil, to oil
$^1/_2$ cup (50g) slivered almonds, lightly toasted
generous 1 cup (250ml) crème anglaise (see page 216), well chilled (see note)

for the caramel

1 cup (200g) superfine sugar

Heat the milk and $^1/_4$ cup (50g) of the sugar in a wide, shallow pan. As soon as it comes to a boil, lower the heat to maintain a temperature of 158–176°F (70–80°C).

In a bowl, beat the egg whites to a thick foam, then shower in the remaining $^3/_4$ cup (140g) sugar and continue to beat until very firm. Using a large spoon, lift out one-quarter of the meringue and shape into a large quenelle on the spoon with the aid of a knife. Dip the spoon into the hot milk; the egg white will slide off into the milk. Rinse the spoon in cold water and repeat to make 4 quenelles or "islands."

Poach the meringue islands for 2 minutes, then delicately turn them over in the milk and poach for 2 minutes on the other side until just firm to the touch, but still delicate and light. Use a skimmer to lift out the islands, one at a time, placing them on a dish towel to drain thoroughly. Transfer the islands to a lightly oiled sheet of foil.

To make the caramel, dissolve the sugar in a small pan, stirring gently and constantly with a wooden spoon. As soon as it turns to a light golden caramel, spoon it over the islands and immediately scatter on the slivered almonds. Pour the chilled crème anglaise into a shallow serving bowl and float the caramelized islands on top. Serve at once, with a bowl of fresh berries if they are in season.

NOTE The crème anglaise should be well flavored with vanilla, so infuse the milk with 2 vanilla beans.

raspberry macaroons

makes about 40

"These delicate little macaroons are very elegant.
Serve them simply with coffee, or with ice cream or sorbet."

$1^{3}/_{4}$ cups (180g) confectioners' sugar, sifted
scant 1 cup (100g) ground almonds
1 tbsp (10g) raspberry powder (see note)
3 egg whites
4 drops of red food coloring
scant $^{1}/_{4}$ cup (40g) superfine sugar

for the raspberry butter
$1^{2}/_{3}$ cups (200g) fresh raspberries
$^{1}/_{4}$ cup (50g) superfine sugar
$6^{1}/_{2}$ tbsp (80g) butter, softened

First make the raspberry butter. Put the raspberries and sugar in a small pan and cook gently for 20 minutes. Whiz in a blender for 1 minute, then pass through a strainer into a bowl. Leave until cold, then gradually whisk into the butter; set aside.

For the macaroons, preheat the oven to 315°F (160°C). Mix together the confectioners' sugar, ground almonds, and raspberry powder. Beat the egg whites in a bowl to a thick foam, then add the red coloring and superfine sugar, and beat for 1 minute until firm. Gradually shower in the almond mixture, folding it in with a spatula until it is amalgamated. Put the mixture into a pastry bag fitted with a plain $^{1}/_{2}$-inch (1-cm) tip.

Pipe about 40 macaroons onto a baking sheet lined with parchment paper, making them $1^{1}/_{4}$–$1^{1}/_{2}$ inches (3–4cm) in diameter and of uniform size. Pipe well apart in staggered rows, so they will cook evenly and won't touch as they spread. Slide the baking sheet onto another one to make a double thickness, and bake for 7 minutes.

Slide the parchment paper onto a wire rack and let cool. When cold, lift the macaroons off the paper and sandwich them together in pairs with raspberry butter.

NOTE If you can't find raspberry powder, you can make your own. Spread fresh raspberries out on a baking sheet lined with parchment paper and dry in a warming oven or airing cupboard for 3 to 4 days. When bone dry, grind the raspberries to a powder in a blender, then rub through a strainer.

genoese sponge

makes an 8-inch (20-cm) sponge cake

Genoese sponge has an excellent texture and many uses. It also freezes well.

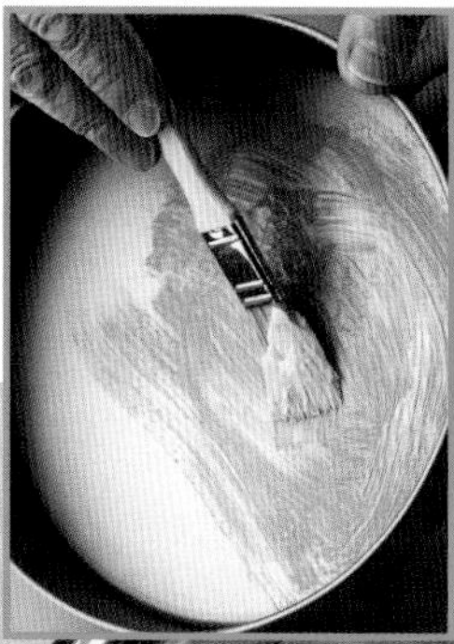

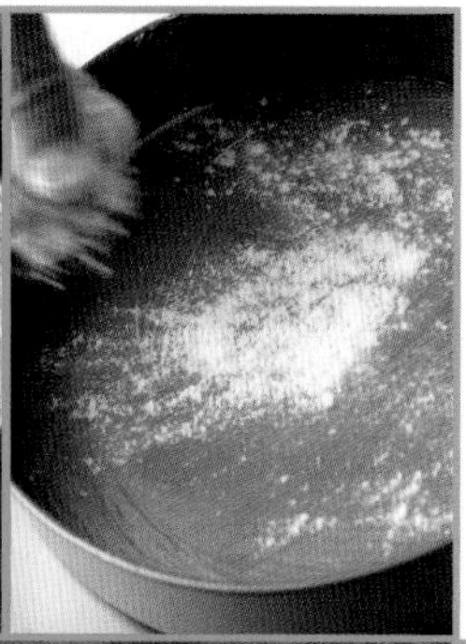

$1\frac{1}{2}$ tbsp (20g) softened butter, to grease pan
scant 1 cup (125g) all-purpose flour, plus extra to dust
4 medium eggs, at room temperature
$\frac{1}{2}$ cup plus 2 tbsp (125g) superfine sugar
2 tbsp butter, melted and cooled to tepid

Preheat the oven to 375°F (190°C). Butter and lightly flour an 8-inch (20-cm) cake pan. Put the eggs and sugar in a bowl and whisk them together.

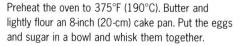

Continue to whisk for about 12 minutes, until the mixture leaves a ribbon trail when you lift the whisk. (You can also do this in an electric mixer.)

Shower in the flour and delicately fold it into the mixture, with a rubber spatula.

Add the melted butter and fold in carefully, without overworking the mixture.

Pour the batter into the cake pan and bake for 30 minutes, or until it is cooked. To test, lightly press the center of the sponge with your fingertips; there should be a slight resistance and the sponge should "sing," emitting a soft "zzzz." Invert onto a wire rack, giving the sponge a quarter-turn after 10 minutes to prevent it sticking. Let cool for 3 to 4 hours.

Chocolate Genoese sponge Replace the scant cup (125 g) flour with a generous $\frac{1}{2}$ cup (75 g) all-purpose flour and $\frac{1}{3}$ cup (50 g) unsweetened cocoa, sifted together, then follow the method for plain Genoese sponge (see page 268).

Uses for Genoese sponge

Using a serrated knife, split the Genoese horizontally into two layers. Sandwich together with buttercream (see page 258) and dust the top with superfine or confectioners' sugar, or top with extra buttercream.

Serve the Genoese plain, cut into thin slices. I love to dunk these in vanilla crème anglaise (see page 216) before eating.

Lamingtons Make 1 quantity of Genoese sponge mixture (see page 268) and cook in a buttered and floured 6-inch (15-cm) square cake pan, which is $1\frac{1}{2}$ inches (4 cm) deep (following the method on page 268). Let cool (and, ideally, store in an airtight pan overnight before frosting).

For the frosting, sift 1 lb (500 g) confectioners' sugar with $\frac{1}{2}$ cup (50 g) unsweetened cocoa into a bowl, then stir in $1\frac{1}{2}$ tbsp (20g) melted butter and $\frac{3}{4}$ cup (175 ml) milk. Stand the bowl over a pan of simmering water and stir until the frosting is smooth and a thin coating consistency. Take the bowl off the pan and leave until the frosting is cold and slightly thickened. Cut the sponge into 1-inch (2.5-cm) squares. Scatter $2\frac{1}{2}$ cups (350 g) dry unsweetened coconut on a board. Working with 4 or 5 sponge squares at a time, dip into the frosting to coat, then roll in the coconut. Leave on a wire rack until set. Serve these little Australian cakes with coffee or tea, or as a dessert with vanilla ice cream (see page 238).

raspberry roulade

makes about 40

"Fragrant raspberries make an ideal filling for this roulade, although wild strawberries are equally good when in season. For sheer decadence, serve with a glass of pink Champagne."

1½ tbsp (20g) softened butter, to grease
flour, to dust
1 quantity Genoese sponge mixture (see page 268)

to finish

confectioners' sugar, to dust

for the filling

1¼ cups (300ml) heavy cream
4oz (100g) crème pâtissière (see page 220)
9oz (250g) jar raspberry jelly, or strained raspberry preserve
1lb (500g) raspberries, hulled

Preheat the oven to 350°F (180°C) Lay a 16 x 12 inches (40 x 30cm) sheet of waxed paper on a baking sheet and lightly butter the paper, then dust lightly with flour. Refrigerate or set aside in a cool place.

Spread the Genoese sponge mixture over the paper in a ½-inch (1-cm) layer. Bake in the oven for 6 to 8 minutes. Immediately cover the cooked sponge with a dish towel and invert it on the dish towel onto a wire rack. Carefully peel off the paper and set aside to cool for 5 minutes only.

Meanwhile, for the filling, whip the cream to a ribbon consistency, then add the crème pâtissière and mix thoroughly with a whisk.

Fill the roulade as soon as it has just cooled, otherwise it will be difficult to roll. Loosen the raspberry jelly with a whisk and spread it delicately over the surface of the sponge. Trim all 4 sides with a serrated knife to neaten and remove the crusty edges. Spread the cream mixture over the surface of the sponge, stopping ½ inch (1cm) short of the edges, then scatter the raspberries over the cream.

Using the dish towel to help you, carefully roll up the sponge from a long side to form a neat roll. Chill for 3 to 4 hours. Dust the roulade with confectioners' sugar to serve.

chocolate truffle cake with candied kumquats

serves 8

"This alluring dessert is always popular and it is simple to make. You can prepare both the cake and kumquats a day or two in advance and keep them in the refrigerator."

1lb 1oz (475g) good-quality semisweet chocolate (70% cocoa solids), chopped into small pieces
1 chocolate Genoese sponge base, 8 inches (20cm) in diameter (see page 268)
splash of cognac or rum
2 cups (475ml) heavy cream
unsweetened cocoa, to dust

for the candied kumquats
16 very ripe kumquats
600g caster sugar

First prepare the kumquats. Put them in a small pan, cover with cold water, and boil for 1 minute, then refresh in cold water. Repeat this twice more; drain. Return to the pan, add 2½ cups (600ml) water and the sugar and slowly bring to a boil. Lower the heat to keep the syrup at 176–194°F (80–90°C) and poach the kumquats for 30 to 45 minutes, until lightly candied. Transfer to a bowl with the syrup and leave until cold.

For the truffle cake, gently melt the chocolate in a bowl over a pan of hot water, then take the bowl off the pan and cool for a few minutes until no less than 77°F (25°C).

Using a serrated knife, cut a ¼-inch (5-mm) thick disk from the chocolate sponge. Place it on a cardboard base and place a pastry ring round the sponge. If the sponge seems dry, moisten with a little of the kumquat syrup, flavored with cognac or rum.

Whip the cream in a large bowl to a ribbon consistency. Fold in half of the melted chocolate with a whisk, then fold in the rest. Whisk very lightly until amalgamated. Pour the mixture into the pastry ring and push it to the edge, taking care not to leave any air holes. Smooth the surface with a knife. Put the truffle cake in the refrigerator for at least 2 hours to firm up.

To serve, warm the pastry ring briefly with a blowtorch or hot cloth, then remove. Dust the cake with cocoa and cut into slices. Serve with the candied kumquats.

sauces & dressings

The classic emulsion sauces—hollandaise, mayonnaise, and sabayon, rely on the unique properties of eggs. Refined, delicate, and airy, hollandaise and sabayon make the most marvelous accompaniments to fish, vegetables, and other dishes. They each take only 10 to 15 minutes to prepare and cook, but they will lose their lightness if kept waiting, so serve within 15 minutes of cooking. Mayonnaise is the key to taste heaven. The addition of snipped fresh herbs, chopped hard-cooked eggs, fresh tomato coulis, or grated horseradish, promotes an explosion of flavors to enhance seafood, smoked fish, hard-cooked eggs, and more. Finally, I use egg yolks to bind and enrich salad dressings, such as my Swiss vinaigrette (see page 296) and Caesar dressing (see page 294), as well as selected sauces (see pages 297–9).

hollandaise sauce **serves 6**

This light, creamy classic has inspired a host of other sauces.

In a pan, mix the wine vinegar with 4 tbsp cold water and the pepper. Reduce by one-third and let cool. Meanwhile, heat the butter in a pan over low heat and slowly bring to a boil. Skim off the froth, then carefully pour the clarified butter into a bowl, leaving the milky sediment behind. Cool until tepid.

1 tbsp white wine vinegar
1 tsp white peppercorns, crushed
2 sticks (250g) butter
4 egg yolks
salt
juice of 1/2 lemon

Add the egg yolks to the cold vinegar reduction and mix with a whisk. Put the pan on a heat diffuser over very low heat and continue whisking, making sure the whisk comes into contact with the bottom of the pan.

Gradually increase the heat so that the sauce emulsifies progressively, becoming smooth and creamy after 8 to 10 minutes. Do not allow the temperature to rise above 149°F (65°C).

Hollandaise cannot be kept waiting, so serve it as soon as it is made, or keep it covered for a short time in a warm place if you must.

Off the heat and still whisking, pour in the tepid clarified butter in a steady stream. Season the sauce with salt. At the last moment, stir in the lemon juice. Pass the sauce through a cheesecloth-lined chinois or strainer to eliminate the crushed peppercorns if required, then serve immediately.

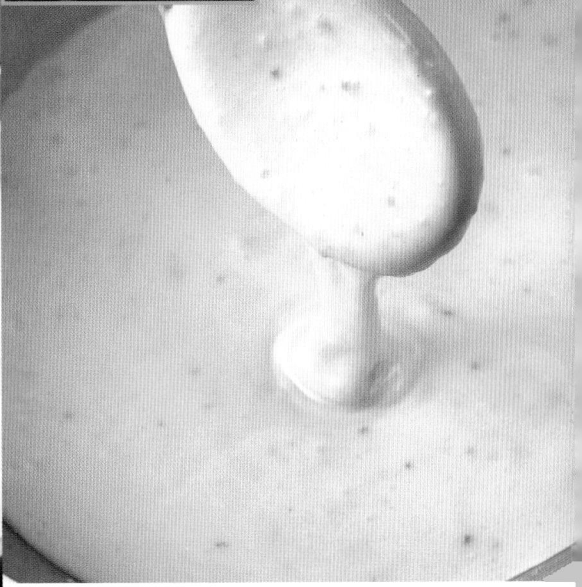

VARIATION To make a noisette sauce, stir 4 tbsp (50 g) foaming browned butter in at the end. This sauce is even more delicate than a hollandaise, and it's particularly good with fish.

mustard hollandaise

serves 6

"This mildly piquant sauce enhances the flavor of salmon without overpowering it. Try it with broiled salmon steaks and samphire (as shown). It's also delicious with steamed zucchini."

5 tbsp (75ml) heavy cream
2 tbsp (30g) strong Dijon mustard
1 quantity freshly made hollandaise sauce (see page 278)
salt and freshly ground pepper

Whip the cream in a bowl to a ribbon consistency, then mix in the mustard until evenly blended.

Whisk the mustard cream little by little into the hollandaise. Season with salt and pepper to taste and serve immediately.

NOTE If preferred, use 1 tbsp English mustard powder dissolved in a few drops of warm water in place of the Dijon mustard.

mayonnaise

makes $1^{1}/_{4}$ cups (300ml)

2 egg yolks, at room temperature
1 tbsp strong Dijon mustard
salt and freshly ground pepper
1 cup (250ml) peanut oil, at room temperature
2 tbsp white wine vinegar or lemon juice

Stand a mixing bowl on a dish towel on the surface. Put the egg yolks, mustard, a little salt, and pepper into the bowl and mix with a balloon whisk.

Slowly add the oil in a thin trickle to begin with, whisking continuously.

Mayonnaise has many uses, but it's especially good with fish and seafood. It can be kept for several hours in a cold place, covered with plastic wrap.

As the mayonnaise begins to thicken, add the oil in a steady stream, still whisking all the time.

When the oil is completely incorporated, whisk more rapidly for 30 seconds, until the mayonnaise is thick and glossy. Add the vinegar or lemon juice, taste, and adjust the seasoning as necessary.

Creamy mayonnaise Stir in 2 tbsp heavy cream after adding the vinegar or lemon juice.

Light mayonnaise For a less rich mayonnaise, simply substitute egg whites for the egg yolks.

Bagnarotte sauce Flavor one quantity of mayonnaise (see page 282) with 3 tbsp tomato ketchup, ½ tsp Worcestershire sauce, 1 tbsp cognac (optional), 2 tbsp heavy cream, 6 drops of Tabasco, and the juice of ½ lemon. Whisk well to combine and season with salt and pepper to taste. Refrigerate until ready to use. This refreshing sauce is delicious with fresh crab, ripe tomatoes, and cucumber, and with poached eggs (see page 44) or hard-cooked eggs (see page 19).

Lowfat mayonnaise In a mixing bowl, whisk ⅔ cup (150 g) fromage blanc or fromage frais (0% fat) with 1 egg yolk, 1 tsp strong Dijon mustard, and 1 tbsp white wine vinegar or lemon juice until completely smooth. Season with salt and pepper to taste. If you wish, stir in a little snipped fresh mint, chives, or tarragon, or some chervil leaves, just before serving.

green mayonnaise

serves 6

"A simple hard-cooked egg with this amazing sauce is a treat. I like to serve it alongside a medley of smoked fish and shellfish (eel, trout, mackerel, oysters, mussels, etc), on toasted baguette slices—as tapas."

1 quantity mayonnaise (see page 282)
salt and freshly ground pepper

for the spinach and herb extract
7oz (200g) spinach, stalks removed
1/4oz (10g) chervil, stalks removed
3/4oz (20g) Italian parsley, stalks removed
1/4oz (10g) tarragon, stalks removed
1/4oz (10g) chives, stalks removed
1/4oz (10g) shallot, thinly sliced

To make the spinach and herb extract, wash and dry the spinach and herb leaves, then put into a blender or electric herb chopper. Add the shallot and 1½ cups (350ml) water and whiz for 1 minute at low speed, then for another 4 minutes at medium speed.

Loosely drape a piece of cheesecloth over a pan and secure it with an elastic band. Pour the herb purée into the cheesecloth and let it drip through slowly. After about 10 minutes, gather up the edges of the cheesecloth and squeeze to extract as much liquid as possible. Discard the herb residue and rinse the cheesecloth in cold water.

Gently heat the green liquid in the pan, stirring delicately with a wooden spoon. As soon as the liquid starts to tremble, take the pan off the heat. Loosely drape the cheesecloth over a bowl and secure with an elastic band. Delicately ladle the green liquid onto the cheesecloth and let drain through for about 20 minutes. Use a spatula to scrape off the soft green mixture from the surface of the cheesecloth and put it into a ramekin. (It will keep for several days in the refrigerator covered with a little peanut oil.)

To make the green mayonnaise, whisk a spoonful or two of the spinach and herb extract into the mayonnaise, to taste. Check the seasoning, then serve.

classic sabayon **serves 4**

You will need a cooking thermometer to check the temperature of the sabayon.

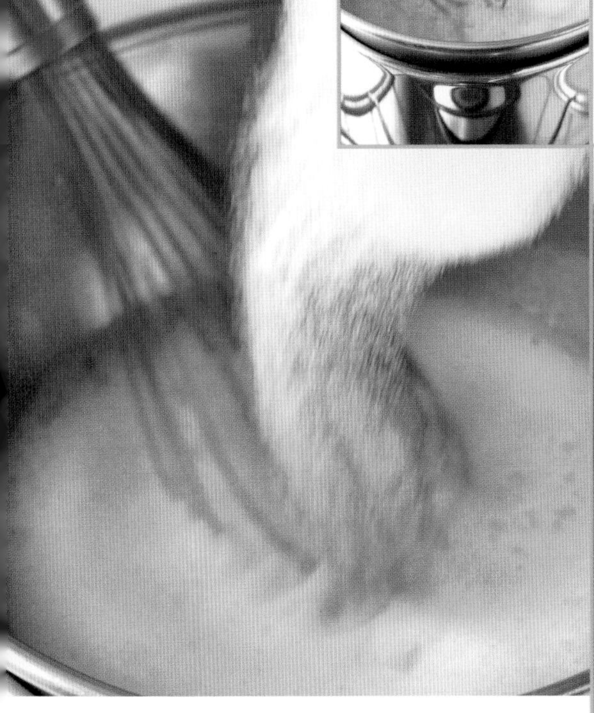

$^1/_3$ cup (100ml) Sauternes or other sweet wine
3 egg yolks
scant $^1/_4$ cup (40g) superfine sugar

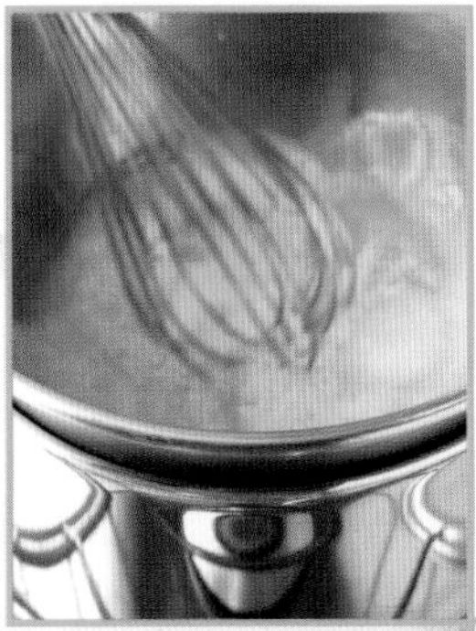

Continue whisking the mixture over the heat so that it gradually thickens, making sure that the temperature of the water in the pan increases steadily but moderately.

Two-thirds fill a pan (large enough to hold a round-bottom bowl) with warm water, and heat gently. Pour the Sauternes into the bowl, then add the egg yolks, whisking as you go. Carry on whisking as you shower in the sugar.

VARIATION Replace the Sauternes with Banyuls or Marsala, or with an eau-de-vie, such as raspberry or pear. For an eau-de-vie sabayon, use 5 tbsp (75ml) eau-de-vie and 4 tbsp (50ml) water, and increase the sugar by 50%.

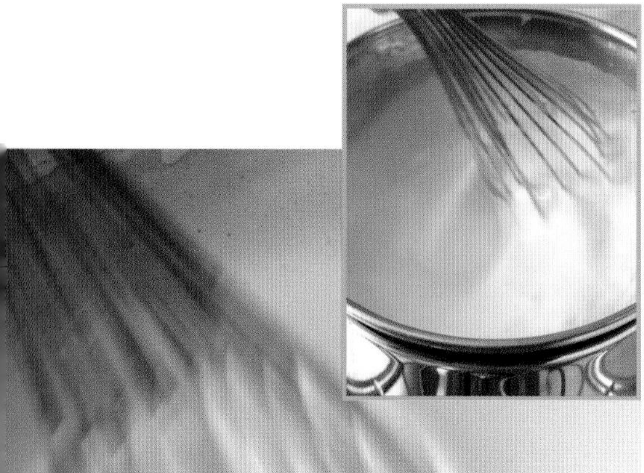

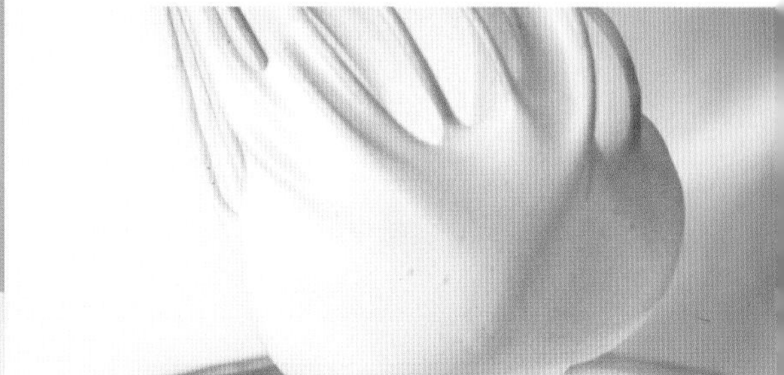

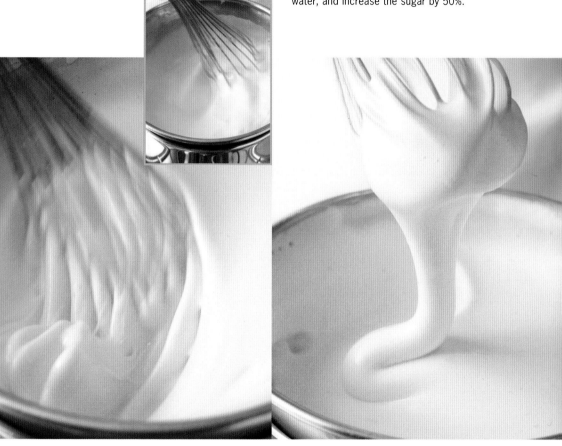

After 8 to 10 minutes, the mixture should have reached a light ribbon consistency. It is essential to keep whisking all the time. When the temperature reaches 131°F (55°C), the sabayon is cooked.

Turn off the heat and continue whisking until the sabayon has a very thick ribbon consistency and a fluffy, rich, and shiny texture. Remove the bowl from the pan. Serve the sabayon immediately, in glasses.

chocolate sabayon

serves 6

"Try serving this sabayon topped with little choux buns sprinkled with a few slivered almonds ... delicious."

3/4 cup (150g) superfine sugar
4 egg yolks
1/2 cup (50g) unsweetened cocoa
finely grated zest of 1 orange

Put the sugar in a small pan with 2/3 cup (150 ml) water and dissolve over low heat, then bring to a boil and immediately turn off the heat. Leave the sugar syrup to cool completely.

Two-thirds fill a pan (large enough to hold a round-bottom bowl) with warm water, and heat gently. Pour the sugar syrup into the bowl, then whisk in the egg yolks.

Continue whisking the mixture over the heat (see page 288), for about 8 to 10 minutes, until the sabayon is a light ribbon consistency. When the sabayon reaches 149°F (65°C), it is ready. Turn off the heat and continue whisking until the sabayon has a very thick ribbon consistency and a fluffy, rich, and shiny texture.

Remove the bowl from the pan, then sprinkle in the cocoa, a little at a time, whisking delicately until it has dissolved. Stir in the grated orange zest without overworking the sabayon.

Spoon the sabayon into glasses and serve immediately.

spinach & watercress sabayon

serves 4

"I use this fresh-tasting sabayon to coat my mollet egg & zucchini tarts, (see left, recipe page 29). It's also good with cauliflower or broccoli, or tossed with spaghetti and sprinkled with Parmesan."

4oz (100g) baby spinach leaves
2oz (50g) watercress leaves
salt and freshly ground pepper
2 egg yolks
3 tbsp (40g) butter, diced

Wash the spinach and watercress leaves, then drain well. Bring generous 1/3 cup (100 ml) lightly salted water to a boil in a pan. Immediately drop in the spinach and watercress leaves, cook for 1 minute, then tip the mixture into a blender and whiz for 1 minute. Pass the purée through a chinois or fine strainer into a small bowl, then set over ice to cool the mixture quickly.

Two-thirds fill a pan (large enough to hold a round-bottom bowl) with warm water, and heat gently. Pour the spinach and watercress purée into the bowl and set over the pan. Add the egg yolks, whisking as you go.

Whisk the mixture constantly for 8 to 10 minutes (see page 288), until it has a light ribbon consistency. When the sabayon reaches 158°F (70°C), it is ready.

Remove the bowl from the pan, then gradually whisk in the diced butter. The sabayon should have a rich, shiny texture. Season with salt and pepper to taste and serve immediately.

NOTE **If preferred, use 1 tbsp English mustard powder dissolved in a few drops of warm water in place of the Dijon mustard.**

caesar dressing

serves 6

1 egg yolk
1/8 tsp Dijon mustard
1 tbsp lemon juice
sliver of garlic, crushed
1 tsp bottled anchovy extract
5 tbsp (75ml) peanut oil
1 oz (30g) Parmesan, freshly grated
freshly ground pepper

Put the egg yolk, mustard, lemon juice, and crushed garlic in a bowl, and blend with a small whisk until very smooth.

Add the anchovy extract, then slowly whisk in the peanut oil until amalgamated. Add the grated Parmesan, and finally whisk in 2 tbsp water to give a slightly looser consistency. Season the dressing with pepper to taste.

"This dressing is particularly good with robust salad greens, such as romaine. It is the dressing used in my Caesar salad with poached eggs (see right, recipe page 55)."

swiss vinaigrette

serves 6

$^3/_4$oz (20g) shallot, finely chopped
$^1/_2$ garlic clove, crushed and chopped
pinch of sugar
1 egg yolk
1 tsp Maggi liquid seasoning (available in supermarkets)
2 tbsp heavy cream
6 tbsp peanut oil
2 tbsp white wine vinegar
salt and freshly ground pepper

Put all the ingredients, except the oil, wine vinegar, salt, and pepper, in a bowl. Mix thoroughly with a whisk for a minute or two, then pour in the peanut oil in a thin steady stream, whisking as you go. Finally, whisk in the wine vinegar and season with salt and pepper to taste.

"I love the flavor of this creamy vinaigrette, which goes perfectly with my mollet eggs on crabmeat & celeriac julienne (see page 32) and mollet eggs with arugula & Parmesan shavings (see page 28). It is also brilliant with a romaine lettuce or escarole salad."

sauce écossaise

serves 4–6

"This sauce is the perfect accompaniment for my poached eggs on potatoes with smoked haddock (see page 51)."

2 tbsp (30g) butter
scant 1/4 cup (30g) all-purpose flour
2 cups (500ml) milk
2 1/4 oz (60g) carrot, finely diced
2 oz (50g) celery, finely diced
2 1/4 oz (60g) green beans, finely diced
2 1/4 oz (50g) onion, finely diced
4 tbsp (50g) butter
1/4 cup (50ml) heavy cream
1 egg yolk
juice of 1 lemon
salt and freshly ground pepper

First make a béchamel. Melt the butter in a small, heavy pan over low heat, then add the flour, stir with a whisk, and cook gently for 2 to 3 minutes to make a white roux. Pour the cold milk onto the roux, as you whisk, and bring to a boil over medium heat, whisking constantly. When the sauce comes to a boil, lower the heat and let simmer gently for about 7 minutes, stirring at regular intervals.

Meanwhile, blanch the vegetables in boiling water for 1 minute. Refresh in cold water, drain, and pat dry. Melt the butter in a small pan, add the blanched vegetables, and let sweat gently for 2 to 3 minutes.

Add the vegetables to the béchamel and let the sauce bubble for 2 to 3 minutes. Mix the cream and egg yolk together, then stir into the sauce. As soon it comes back to a boil, stir in the lemon juice, and remove from the heat. Season the sauce with salt and pepper to taste. It is now ready to serve.

NOTE For an egg gratin, arrange sliced hard-cooked eggs in a well-buttered ovenproof dish, coat thickly with sauce écossaise, and heat in the oven at 350°F (180°C) for 5 minutes.

mornay sauce

serves 4–6

2 tbsp (30g) butter
scant ¼ cup (30g) all-purpose flour
2 cups (500ml) milk
pinch of freshly grated nutmeg
salt and freshly ground white pepper
3 egg yolks
¼ cup (50ml) heavy cream
4oz (100g) Gruyère, Emmental, or Cheddar, finely grated

First make a béchamel. Melt the butter in a small, heavy pan over low heat, then add the flour, stir with a whisk, and cook gently for 2 to 3 minutes to make a white roux. Pour the cold milk onto the roux, as you whisk, and bring to a boil over medium heat, whisking constantly. When the sauce comes to a boil, lower the heat, and let simmer gently for about 10 minutes, stirring frequently. Season to taste with nutmeg, salt, and white pepper.

Mix the egg yolks and cream together in a bowl, then pour the mixture into the béchamel, whisking as you do so. Let the sauce bubble for about 1 minute, whisking constantly, then take the pan off the heat and shower in the grated cheese. Stir until melted, then taste and adjust the seasoning if necessary.

"Coat broccoli with this sauce and top with cheese (see left) for a tasty vegetable dish. I also use it for my poached eggs florentine (see page 48), to make macaroni cheese, and in my chicken & mushroom crêpes (see page 175)."

index

acknowledgments

My thanks are due to the following people, without whom this book would never have seen the light of day:
My son, Alain, who supported and inspired me through many long days and evenings, in both the kitchen and the office.
Chris Lelliott, my number one sous-chef at The Waterside Inn, who helped me to prepare the finished dishes for the photographs with immaculate expertise.
Martin Brigdale, whose magic touch, enthusiasm, and camaraderie produced such amazing photographs of eggs in all their forms.
Mary Evans, who manages to extract from me precisely what she wants. She is a star!
Kate Whiteman, who translates my French manuscripts into English with proficiency. She understands me through and through …
Janet Illsley, for calmly pulling together all the threads amid the melee of author, translator, photographer, artistic director, and the rest …
Mr Secker, of Hard-to-find-farm, High Wycombe, Bucks, who has supplied me with superb organic eggs for many years.
Claude Grant, my assistant, who gives her time when she has none to spare, to type, and fine-tune my French manuscript—pure exploitation!
Robyn Roux, my wife, who patiently puts up with my mood swings and checks the English version of all my recipes and introductory texts.

USEFUL WEBSITES

The two specialist stores listed below have supplied me for many years and are among the best in Europe:
MORA (for kitchen equipment): www.mora.fr
Valrhona (for fine-quality chocolate): www.valrhona.com
For further information about eggs, look up the following websites:
American Egg Board: www.aeb.org
Egg Nutrition Center: www.enc-online.org